HOW TO BUILD NONPERFORMING LOAN TRADING PLATFORMS IN ASIA AND THE PACIFIC

ISSUES AND PROCESSES

MAY 2024

ASIAN DEVELOPMENT BANK

ADB

Contents

Tables, Figures, and Boxes

Foreword

The global economy continues to grapple with ongoing weaknesses amidst geopolitical tensions and tight financial conditions, despite relatively robust growth in developing Asia—forecast at 4.9% in 2024. If global interest rates stay higher for longer than anticipated, they will be a growing burden on debt servicing costs of the public sector and raise refinancing and solvency risks of vulnerable companies in the private sector, which could translate into worsening asset quality in the financial sector.

The rise in nonperforming loans (NPLs) in some countries in Asia and the Pacific could destabilize banking sectors and impede economic recovery efforts unless managed effectively. The recent increase in bad debt write-offs indicates growing financial stress. Preemptive action, including advancing international financial architecture for fairer debt resolution and developing a robust NPL trading market could help address these challenges.

The pandemic has accelerated the adoption of digital solutions globally. Digital technology has transformed financial systems, enhancing efficiency and transparency by facilitating information flows, reducing operational costs, and promoting financial inclusion.

In diverse Asian financial landscapes, online NPL trading platforms provide policymakers with opportunities for efficient and transparent market development for NPL transactions. These platforms can streamline trading processes, overcome obstacles hindering smooth operations, and facilitate larger investment.

In light of these considerations, the Asian Development Bank published the first report to assess the readiness of Asian countries for establishing an NPL trading platform in 2022. Building on the insights of that report, this report focuses on the technical, legal, and regulatory details required to successfully address the challenges of establishing an NPL trading platform. It considers selected country cases, including the Republic of Korea and Viet Nam. The report proposes a standardized data template and provides guidelines for NPL trading platforms.

I trust this report will serve as a valuable reference for advancing financial infrastructure and NPL markets in the region. I hope that the proposed road map can help guide policy actions aimed at bolstering regional NPL markets and enhancing financial stability.

Albert Park
Chief Economist and Director General
Economic Research and Development Impact Department
Asian Development Bank

Acknowledgments

This report was prepared by the Regional Cooperation and Integration Division of the Economic Research and Development Impact Department of the Asian Development Bank (ADB). Report development was supported by TA 9497: Strengthening Asia's Financial Safety Nets and Resolution Mechanisms, financed by ADB's technical assistance special fund, the People's Republic of China Poverty Reduction and Regional Cooperation Fund, and the Republic of Korea e-Asia and Knowledge Partnership Fund. Report production was supported by TA 10180: Asia's Financial Safety Net, Resolution Mechanisms, and Financial Integration and Resilience, financed by ADB's technical assistance special fund and the Republic of Korea e-Asia and Knowledge Partnership Fund.

Under the overall direction and guidance of the Regional Cooperation and Integration Division Director, Jong Woo Kang, Inyoung Hwang, Alexander Raabe, and Paulo Rodelio Halili led preparation of the report with administrative support from Marilyn Parra and Lilibeth Perez. The main authors of the report are Burkhard Heppe (NPL Markets Ltd.), Sungmee Hong, and Nguyen Ngoc Sang (Lee & Ko).

The report team acknowledges helpful support and comments from discussions with the Agency of the Republic of Kazakhstan for Regulation and Development of Financial Markets, Korea Asset Management Corporation, State Bank of Viet Nam, Viet Nam Asset Management Company, Viet Nam Distressed Asset Trading Company, and Zheshang Asset Management Company. Discussions were also held with the European Bank for Reconstruction and Development, the International Finance Corporation, and the World Bank.

The report team is likewise grateful for feedback from Peter Rosenkranz and the participants in the 7th International Public Asset Management Companies Forum Summit and International Conference on 21 September 2023 in Bali, Indonesia.

Eric Van Zant edited the manuscript. Alvin Tubio implemented the typesetting and layout of the report. Mike Cortes created the cover design and typeset the figures and tables. Jess Alfonso Macasaet proofread the report, while Marjorie Celis handled page proof checking, with assistance from Carol Ongchangco and Paulo Rodelio Halili. The Printing Services Unit of ADB's Corporate Services Department and the Publishing Team of the Department of Communications and Knowledge Management supported printing and publishing.

Abbreviations

ABS	asset-backed security
ADB	Asian Development Bank
AI	artificial intelligence
AMC	asset management company
AML	anti-money laundering
B2B	business to business
B2C	business to consumer
COVID-19	coronavirus disease
DATC	Debt and Asset Trading Corporation (Viet Nam)
EBA	European Banking Authority
GDP	gross domestic product
IPAF	International Public Asset Management Companies Forum
KAMCO	Korea Asset Management Corporation
KYC	know your customer
NPL	nonperforming loan
PRC	People's Republic of China
RICS	Royal Institution of Chartered Surveyors
SaaS	software as a service
Sareb	The Company for the Management of Assets from Bank Restructuring (Spain)
SBV	State Bank of Vietnam
SMEs	small and medium-sized enterprises
US	United States
VAMC	Vietnam Asset Management Company
VAT	value added tax
VDR	virtual data room

Glossary

Asset servicers	Support services related to NPL resolution, such as lawyers; accountants; billing, payment collection; or other ancillary services.
Asset and/or loan sale platform	Internet website or web-based application designed to conduct all or portions of the steps to sell assets/loans to a third party.
Auction	Sale of property in a public forum, involving open and competitive bidding.
Data room (physical)	Physical location in which key documents, such as loan agreements, financial data, payment records, etc., are located and available for inspection by all potential investors who have signed a nondisclosure agreement to participate in asset/loan sale.
Data tape (also loan data tape)	An electronic file or set of files that captures information regarding the loan, borrower, and collateral information of the objects for sale.
Due diligence	A comprehensive review, performed by a potential buyer to confirm the facts or details of the assets/loans offered for sale to determine the price the potential buyer is willing to pay.
Dutch auction	A price discovery process in which the auctioneer starts with the highest asking price and lowers it until a bid is received. A Dutch auction is also known as a descending price auction or a uniform price auction.
Electronic Debt Trading Platform	Computer software program used to buy and sell loans (performing or nonperforming) over the internet, either with a financial intermediary, such as an asset management company, or directly between the participants or members of the trading platform. Such platforms provide secure online loan sale execution that allows posting of loans for sale, advertising and marketing, a secure virtual data room for investor due diligence, an online investor question and answer forum, and an online bid platform and closing of sale.
English auction	An ascending dynamic auction which opens with a low starting price that increases as buyers bid for the item until the one willing to pay the highest price wins.
Nondisclosure agreement	A contract by which one or more parties agree not to disclose confidential information that they have shared with each other as a necessary part of the due diligence process. If one party to the agreement fails to uphold its promise, the other party has the option to exercise its legal rights and remedies as specified in the contract, including but not limited to recovering damages for any breach of the contract.
Virtual data room	Secure data sharing website in which key documents such as loan agreements, financial data, payment records, etc., are located and available for inspection by all potential investors who have signed a nondisclosure agreement to participate in asset/loan sale.

Executive Summary

The global landscape is marked by uncertainties stemming from the coronavirus disease pandemic, the Russian invasion of Ukraine, and economic challenges in the People's Republic of China (PRC). These factors, coupled with higher debt levels and monetary tightening, are potential risks for Asia's financial systems. Resulting higher nonperforming loans (NPLs) could destabilize banking systems.

As such, to facilitate efficient and timely resolution of NPLs, the Asian Development Bank and the International Public Asset Management Companies Forum are exploring a project to strengthen Asia's NPL markets through electronic trading platforms, aiming to facilitate domestic transfers and cross-border transactions between International Public Asset Management Companies Forum members and investors across Asia and the Pacific.

Information asymmetry, bid–offer gaps, and coordination issues hinder efficient NPL trading. Transaction platforms can bridge these shortcomings by providing transparency, fostering wider investor participation, and addressing coordination challenges, ultimately enhancing market liquidity.

In Asia and the Pacific, existing platforms focus on their respective domestic markets: private NPL trading platforms operate in the PRC, a public online asset auction platform has operated successfully in the Republic of Korea, and Viet Nam is building a state-owned NPL trading platform. But both private and public platforms can coexist, helping overcome market failures by promoting transparency.

This second feasibility study follows the road map report in 2022 and aligns with the Asian Development Bank's Strategy 2030 aimed at achieving a prosperous, inclusive, resilient, and sustainable Asia and the Pacific. It focuses on implementation details for selected countries, including the Republic of Korea and Viet Nam. Building on these, the study explores technical, legal, and regulatory challenges that need to be addressed before establishing an NPL trading platform.

Efficient NPL trading requires prerequisites like a strong creditor rights framework, information disclosure, good accounting practices, and an effective asset transfer framework. Addressing legal and regulatory barriers is crucial. The proposed electronic NPL trading platforms hold promise in enhancing Asia's financial stability by addressing market inefficiencies, promoting transparency, and encouraging wider investor participation.

Platforms Reduce Barriers to Nonperforming Loan Trading

The report offers insights into the features, good practices, and general design principles of NPL transaction platforms. It highlights the varied nature of these platforms, categorized as retail-focused or institutional, each catering to different user bases and assets. Platforms can be publicly or privately owned, subject to specific or generic laws, and may focus on single assets or portfolios with different transfer values.

The core services of NPL trading platforms include facilitating transactions, providing data services, operating as a data hub, offering ancillary services like valuation tools, and supporting payment and settlement.

While specific regulations governing NPL platforms are absent globally, Kazakhstan is implementing an accreditation process. Existing rules for auction platforms generally apply to all platforms while additional regulations for multilateral trading facilities or alternative trading systems apply depending on local rules and platform activities. Information only platforms may not be subject to specific regulation while platforms offering online execution and settlement will be subject to greater regulatory scrutiny.

The report outlines good business practices for NPL platforms, emphasizing compliance with legal standards and market conventions. It discusses the main activities necessary for a successful transaction process, including transaction structuring, data preparation, bidding processes, signing of transfer documents, and pre- and post-auction activities.

General principles for NPL trading platforms emphasize accessibility, transparency, data integrity, security, and support for key execution steps which include user registration, data preparation, nondisclosure agreements, virtual data rooms for due diligence, auction execution, communication tools, help desk, and complaints procedures.

Insights into Asian Nonperforming Loan Market and Platform Activities

According to Deloitte estimates, Asia and the Pacific had $707 billion in NPLs at the end of 2022, with the PRC holding the largest share, at $432 billion, followed by Japan ($104 billion). The PRC's NPL market, likewise, is one of the world's largest, exceeding $100 billion in annual trades and growing despite recent challenges (Deloitte 2023).

In the PRC, various tools are employed for NPL resolution, such as write-offs, debt restructuring, legal enforcement, portfolio sales, and securitization. The NPL market is active, with online auction platforms playing a significant role.

In the Republic of Korea, the NPL market has matured. The Korea Asset Management Corporation has actively resolved NPLs in line with government policy, and recent NPL acquisitions have increased. The Korea Asset Management Corporation also operates the online asset auction platform OnBid, a dedicated channel for the sale of state-owned, foreclosed, or entrusted properties, with a focus on real estate and movable assets.

In Viet Nam, despite a healthy economy—inflation below target and gross domestic product growth of 5%—real estate market stress doubled the NPL ratio in 2023. Viet Nam's debt markets are in an earlier stage of development than the PRC's or the Republic of Korea's. The country's online NPL trading platform, the Loan Transaction Platform Branch of Vietnam Asset Management Company, initiated in October 2021, aims to resolve bad debts and promote debt market development. But it needs to attract more buyers and sellers and to improve the legal framework.

The success of NPL trading platforms depends on a supportive framework, including a robust creditor rights system, transparent bidding mechanisms, and access to information for investors. The platforms aim to streamline asset disposal processes, enhance transparency, and reduce transaction costs. Platforms provide comprehensive details of NPLs, fostering efficient communication between buyers and sellers. They leverage big data for informed decision-making and valuation, optimize operational efficiencies, and reduce transaction fees. However, challenges persist due to the complex nature of NPLs, often requiring offline communication for negotiation and due diligence. In the PRC and the Republic of Korea, existing online platforms lack specialization tailored to complex NPLs, limiting engagement from institutional investors.

Internal platforms operated by major sellers are suitable for long-term, large-scale operations, but they are time-consuming and costly to establish. External platforms offer ready-to-use solutions, access to diverse investor bases, and operational experience but may incur higher fees for extended use. The decisions to buy or build a platform hinge on factors like the scale of operations and need for customization.

Legal and Regulatory Challenges in Nonperforming Loan Trading in Viet Nam and the Republic of Korea

The report details the crucial dimensions of the legal and regulatory environment necessary for effective NPL trading platforms in Asia and the Pacific, focusing on the Republic of Korea and Viet Nam. It compares international benchmarks of judicial and NPL workout efficiencies, highlighting that countries with more efficient and modern insolvency frameworks tend to have shorter resolution times and higher recovery rates.

In the Republic of Korea, a well-established legal system deals with NPL resolution including NPL securitizations. The Korea Asset Management Corporation is crucial in restructuring NPLs and supporting the recovery of insolvent businesses. Viet Nam's NPL resolution mechanism is evolving, allowing debt trading through direct negotiation and auctions, with no regulation covering securitization. The legal framework is still developing, with significant progress, including the establishment of asset management companies.

Data Requirements and Valuation

This report explores data requirements for trading and valuing NPLs, acknowledging the complexity of valuing NPLs due to their unique characteristics. The discussion covers various datasets necessary for informed decision-making, the impact of data on different valuation methodologies, and the role of NPL transaction platforms in data preparation and validation.

Investors need diverse data for informed decisions on NPL purchases, including loan borrower and collateral information, historical performance data, legal documents, communication records, and market data. Credit risk information, such as credit reports and scoring models, is crucial for assessing borrower creditworthiness and viability. Historical recovery rates, time to recovery, and collateral valuations are key inputs in valuing NPLs.

Different valuation methods include the market approach (comparable sales), income approach (discounted cash flow), historical recovery rates, and scenario analysis. The choice of valuation method depends on data availability, NPL complexity, and specific circumstances.

In Asia and the Pacific, there is no standardized data template for NPL transactions. Many banks and asset management companies rely on external valuation advisors for asset valuations and, less commonly, for NPL valuations. A robust due diligence process, involving comprehensive data and document analysis, is crucial for understanding challenges and opportunities in NPL investments. NPL transaction platforms can play an important role in facilitating data preparation, validation, and automated valuation.

A Proposed Data Template for Asia and the Pacific

As part of this feasibility study, a proposed data template draws on international experience and focuses on portfolio sales to institutional investors. Business-to-consumer auction platforms selling single assets or single NPLs are not expected to use these templates. The proposed data template for Asia and the Pacific is based on the European Banking Authority NPL data templates with some adjustments. Certain data fields have been added based on user feedback from Asian investors: for instance, as many Asian countries do not allow freehold ownership of land, the expiry date of land lease rights is an important data field in Asia and the Pacific not present in the European template.

Standardized data templates ease the design and implementation of detailed automated data quality checks. Such checks are crucial for ensuring the reliability and accuracy of data populated into the template and available NPL trading platform. High-quality data fosters trust among users and keeps due diligence costs manageable.

Standardized data templates help market participants understand the important data requirement in an NPL transaction. Standard templates will only help the market become more efficient if use is widespread or mandatory. Sellers know that a certain minimum information set is required from them, and buyers can easily understand and automatically process and value loan portfolios based on standardized data, making a successful sale more likely and faster to execute. For complex loans or assets, the data tape, even if comprehensive and of good quality, will not in itself be sufficient to execute a trade successfully. Investors need to conduct detailed legal and financial due diligence, requiring access to unstructured information outside the data tapes, which are typically provided in a virtual data room. The valuation of an NPL can be complex and some NPL transaction platforms provide powerful self-service valuation tools.

Blueprint for Nonperforming Loan Trading Platforms: Key Functions, Business Models, Best Practices, and Ancillary Services

The report offers a blueprint for establishing an NPL transaction platform in Asia and the Pacific, drawing on prior international experience. Three types of platforms are discussed: information-only platforms, trading systems, and data hubs. The report suggests a gradual approach to establishing a regional platform in Asia and the Pacific, accommodating varying market development stages across jurisdictions. It also discusses the idea of a network of regional platforms with shared standards to optimize efficiency and market reach.

The discussion of key functions covers platform fees, emphasizing transparency, affordability, and the need for critical mass for the platform to operate effectively. The various fee elements include registration, listing, transaction, data preparation, a virtual data room, cybersecurity, and software-as-a service subscription fees.

The benefits for sellers and buyers in using NPL transaction platforms are highlighted, including wider market access, lower transaction costs, transparent pricing, and process efficiency. The study underscores the potential for supervisors to incentivize platform use through regulatory capital relief, performance-based incentives, and enhanced reporting and data sharing.

Ancillary Platform Services

Additional services for NPL platforms include transaction advisory, data preparation, valuation, stress testing, deal closing, and reporting. These services enhance analytical capacity and facilitate smoother debt trading.

Implementing an effective marketing and sales strategy involves identifying the target audience, developing a compelling value proposition, highlighting benefits, providing case studies, building a strong brand, using targeted advertising, leveraging content marketing, attending industry events, creating referral programs, and measuring results.

Possible Challenges of Online Nonperforming Loan Trading Platforms

The report concludes with the description of some challenges of online NPL platforms. While trading platforms are essential tools, they may not address all challenges in NPL sales. Strong service offerings are crucial. Setting up a new platform can be time-consuming and costly, and existing solutions should be considered. Critical factors include cybersecurity, ease of use, and a user-friendly interface. Hybrid models and partnerships with third-party advisors and existing platform or technology providers can enhance efficiency.

1 Introduction

everal factors have undermined confidence in global financial conditions, including the aftermath of the coronavirus disease (COVID-19) pandemic and the Russian invasion of Ukraine. Likewise, there was global monetary tightening after sharp increases in inflation due to higher energy and food prices and supply chain bottlenecks as COVID-19 restrictions waned. Recent stresses in the People's Republic of China (PRC) economy and property market are fueling uncertainty. Higher debt levels in many countries, higher lending rates, a strong United States (US) dollar, weaker real estate markets, and deteriorating credit quality have aggravated the situation, putting the region's financial systems at risk. An increase in nonperforming loans (NPLs) could destabilize banking and financial systems in Asia and the Pacific. Yet, a developed market for NPL trading could help reduce banking system NPLs by mobilizing private capital to relieve distressed bank assets. NPL transaction platforms can help the market develop by connecting sellers with more buyers and overcoming information asymmetries, with platforms acting as data warehouses and enforcing use of standardized and validated data.

The motivation for NPL transaction platforms can be summarized as follows. When banks offer NPLs for sale rather than working them out themselves, potential investors cannot be sure that the credit quality of the assets is as good as the banks portray it to be. Such information asymmetries in the NPL market create a bid–offer gap between the prices that investors are prepared to pay for NPLs and the prices that banks are prepared to sell them for. While information asymmetries can be overcome through investor due diligence, this requires specialist expertise and the costs of valuing NPL portfolios can be high. As few investors have the resources to absorb such costs, barriers to entering the market are compounded (Fell et al. 2017). The result can be a lack of investors (especially foreign) willing to enter a market or a concentration of market power among limited investors, pushing traded prices lower. By offering the prospect of greater transparency in NPL markets, fostering wider investor participation, and addressing coordination issues, NPL transaction platforms could help in overcoming all of these market failures. The resulting improvement in market liquidity would allow banks to achieve better prices for NPL sales, preserve their capital, and mitigate financial stability risks.

While there are good reasons to use NPL transaction platforms to make the market for trading distressed assets more efficient, the reasons for a single state-owned transaction platform are less stringent. State interference in the distressed asset sale ecosystem may be justified to overcome market failure, for instance, where the ecosystem lacks critical components that private market players are unable or unwilling to provide. State interference is often required to establish mandatory transparency rules as a lack of transparency may favor a few large incumbent market players and may decrease competition. Other rules which require changes in legislation or regulation are the mandatory use of standard data templates to improve data availability and data quality, mandatory delivery of transaction data to a central data hub, or the mandatory use of transaction platforms, as Kazakhstan has recently introduced.

State interference can help establish new technology (e.g., improving data protection and cybersecurity or encouraging the use of digital signatures), innovative solutions (e.g., by clarifying the use of generative artificial intelligence [AI] tools during due diligence in smart virtual data rooms [VDR]), and best business practices. State interference can also aim to prevent large technology companies exerting too much market power through their vast datasets on private individuals. For example, the market for judicial auctions in the PRC is dominated by big tech companies like Alibaba acting through its Taobao subsidiary.

State-owned platforms established by the Korea Asset Management Corporation (KAMCO) are created to deal with public sector asset holdings, but no market exists in which use of a central public NPL platform is mandatory for all NPL sales. And in countries where public platforms exist, use of private platforms is also possible.

In the PRC, private platforms act both in the primary market between banks and public asset management companies (AMCs) as well as in the secondary market where AMCs sell to private investors. Taobao is successful in the PRC in auctioning assets thanks to the huge private user base. Taobao also sells NPLs, but the bulk of its activity is sales of assets to individuals, whereas other Chinese platforms, like 360pai, target institutional NPL investors and operate on a smaller scale than the subsidiary of the big consumer tech companies. When assessing a future ecosystem for NPL sales, it is important to maintain a balance between state interference and market freedom so that the market does not become overregulated, which can stifle competition and reduce market participation. The state should encourage market competition and should not have a monopoly on any electronic platform for the sale of NPL.

The Asian Development Bank (ADB) and the International Public Asset Management Companies Forum (IPAF) are collaborating on a project to strengthen Asia's NPL markets through considering an electronic NPL trading platform. This platform would not only allow domestic transfers of NPLs but may also enable cross-border transactions between IPAF members and investors. For this purpose, an IPAF Research Committee on an Asian Online NPL Trading Platform was established in 2020.

ADB's first feasibility study (ADB 2022), completed in 2022, assessed the readiness of countries in Asia and the Pacific for establishing an NPL trading platform. Building on the general insights of the first study, this second study focuses on implementation details for selected countries including the Republic of Korea and Viet Nam, identifying technical, legal, and regulatory challenges that need to be addressed prior to establishing an NPL trading platform.

The current study is well aligned with ADB's Strategy 2030 and the mission of IPAF to strengthen crisis response mechanisms through cooperation among members, together contributing to the economic and financial stability of developing member countries. The study aligns with ADB's operational priorities of strengthening governance and institutional capacity as well as fostering regional cooperation and integration.[1]

In this research report, the remainder of this chapter reviews how platforms can reduce barriers to NPL trading. It highlights features of electronic debt trading platforms. Chapter 2 details NPL market and platform activities in Viet Nam and the Republic of Korea and compares them drawing on further examples from the PRC and Kazakhstan. Chapter 3 explains legal and regulatory issues in NPL trading and platform operations, focusing on Viet Nam and the Republic of Korea. Chapter 4 describes the data requirements for NPL trading and valuation and the benefits of a standardized data template for NPL transactions in Asia and the Pacific.

---

[1]   Strategy 2030 envisions a prosperous, inclusive, resilient, and sustainable Asia and the Pacific, while sustaining efforts to eradicate extreme poverty.

As part of this study, the report proposes a standardized data template for Asia based on international experience and feedback from market participants. Finally, Chapter 5 offers a blueprint for NPL trading platforms encompassing the key functions, business models, regulatory analysis, best practices, and ancillary services.

Recommendations on how to make the local market for NPLs more efficient and improve the existing NPL trading platform conclude the report.

1.1 Reducing Barriers to Efficient Nonperforming Loan Trade

For an effective NPL sale, prerequisites include a strong creditor rights framework, adequate disclosure of information, use of good practices in accounting and asset valuation, an effective asset transfer framework, and a conducive tax regime for asset transfers. NPL transaction platforms should help reduce the barriers for investors to enter the market for distressed assets. However, the ability of such platforms to help make the market more efficient depends on addressing the prerequisites and the removal of barriers in the legal and regulatory environment. In addition, even if such market barriers are removed, an efficient market might still not develop, as buyers and sellers may still be unable to overcome wide bid–offer spreads.

For instance, in Viet Nam, the International Finance Corporation has identified several market and valuation barriers (IFC 2022). Bid–offer spreads can be significant in any NPL market. Again, in Viet Nam many NPLs have been transferred at par value of the claims, which may deter specialist distressed debt funds that seek a higher return. The International Finance Corporation identified a lack of appraisal standards for NPLs as a barrier to efficiently pricing the distressed assets in the country. Where the legal status of a loan is not known, the investor will apply additional haircuts to the bidding price.

1.2 First Feasibility Study and Road Map Report

In October 2022, ADB published the *Road Map for Developing an Online Platform to Trade Nonperforming Loans in Asia and the Pacific* following the first phase of a feasibility study conducted in 2021 and 2022 (ADB 2022). The first feasibility study showed an online NPL trading platform could help develop NPL markets by bringing together buyers, sellers, and service providers in a digital marketplace. A trading platform could streamline the overall transaction process and address some supply-side, demand-side, and structural impediments weighing on smooth NPL market function. The first phase focused on the following:

(i) The state and level of development of Asia's NPL markets.

(ii) The benefits, functions, and practical considerations of an electronic NPL trading platform.

(iii) The region's readiness for an electronic platform.

The first feasibility study identified the PRC, the Republic of Korea, and Thailand as countries with relatively high readiness scores for operating online transaction platforms. The first feasibility study identified Viet Nam as having a lower readiness score in that area. The study noted the Government of Viet Nam's interest in improving the legal framework to help the NPL market develop and opening the Vietnam Asset Management Company (VAMC)–Loan Transaction Platform Branch in 2022, aimed at both domestic and international buyers.

1.3 Second Feasibility Study

This second feasibility study extends the first study by assessing technical and operational features for NPL transaction platforms in Asia and the Pacific. It focuses on cross-border opportunities and challenges for investors to enter the local NPL market covering technical, legal, and regulatory aspects and for international transaction platforms to extend their services in jurisdictions under consideration. The study provides an implementation guide for an online NPL trading platform, with specific recommendations for how sellers, buyers, and service providers can interact through the platform. It considers, among other things, the data requirements of market participants and the traded NPLs, best practice guidance on efficient transaction process, and meeting confidentiality and personal data protection requirements.

The current study considers several countries in Asia and the Pacific, focusing, as noted, on the Republic of Korea and Viet Nam, both with online platforms. Both platforms are owned and operated by public AMCs (KAMCO and VAMC, respectively) active in the IPAF group and have made detailed contribution to this study. The study also benefits from work completed by the World Bank as part of two technical assistance programs (World Bank 2022). The World Bank surveyed AMCs to explore issues in electronic debt trading platforms. The report identified KAMCO and the Ukraine Deposit Guarantee Fund as two AMCs actively using trading platforms for disposing real estate assets or NPLs. This feasibility study summarizes the activities of other Asian NPL trading platforms, including in the PRC and Kazakhstan, and provides additional detail on the trading platform in Viet Nam.

The legal and regulatory impediments to NPL trading and the general readiness of selected Asian countries have been discussed in the first road map report. Chapter 3 details the legal and regulatory framework of NPL trading and online platforms and compares the framework in Viet Nam with that in the Republic of Korea, which has a well-developed market for NPL trading and securitizations.

This second feasibility study benefits from a feasibility and methodology study conducted by the European Bank for Reconstruction and Development with the support of KPMG on establishing an NPL trading platform in Kazakhstan (the Kazakhstani Methodology Report, KPMG 2023). The Kazakhstani Methodology Report provides regulatory guidance on how the financial authority can accredit the activities of NPL trading platforms in Kazakhstan.

1.4 Features of Online Nonperforming Loan Trading Platforms and Good Practices

Online platforms can improve NPL secondary markets by encouraging sell-side and buy-side processes for NPL transactions, which are aligned with the good practices found internationally in Europe, the US, and Asia. This section reviews key features, good business practices, and general design principles for setting up and operating an online NPL trading platform.

Features: Platform functions vary by target market (user base and assets traded) and ancillary features (Figure 1). Platforms can be publicly or privately owned and subject to specific laws and regulations or covered by generic laws like other software services, cloud providers or auction sites. Platforms can be retail-focused and organized as websites that showcase the assets for sale like residential real estate listing websites (zillow.com, rightmove.co.uk, or idealista.com).

Platforms can also be retail-focused auction websites like eBay or Taobao/Ali Auction. Further, platforms can be focused on institutional trades only and sell distressed assets to investors on an invitation-only basis. Retail platforms tend to focus on single assets such as residential property and movable collateral items like cars whereas institutional platforms focus on portfolios of loans or assets with higher transfer values compared to retail platforms. Whereas asset sales on retail platforms average below $100,000 and rarely exceed $5 million, institutional platforms have transfer values typically exceeding $1 million. Portfolios can be unsecured claims only or any type of retail or wholesale secured or unsecured loan portfolios.

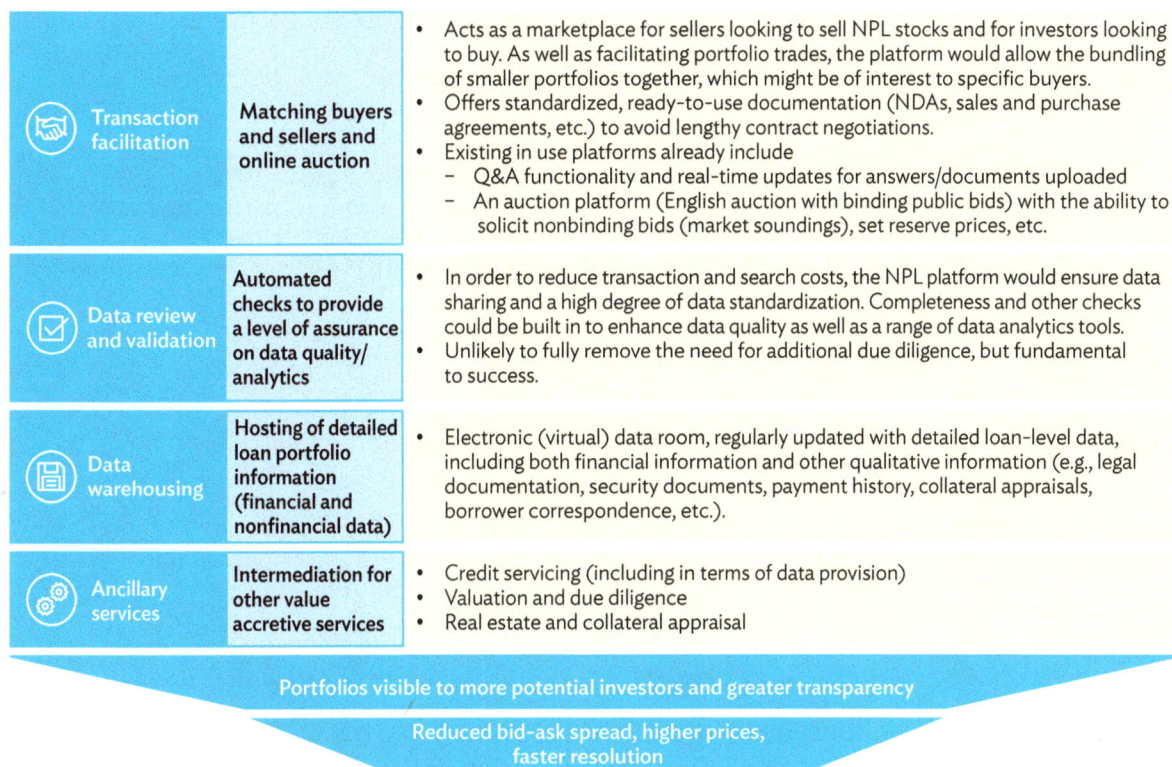

Figure 1: Nonperforming Loan Platform Functionalities

Transaction facilitation	Matching buyers and sellers and online auction	• Acts as a marketplace for sellers looking to sell NPL stocks and for investors looking to buy. As well as facilitating portfolio trades, the platform would allow the bundling of smaller portfolios together, which might be of interest to specific buyers. • Offers standardized, ready-to-use documentation (NDAs, sales and purchase agreements, etc.) to avoid lengthy contract negotiations. • Existing in use platforms already include – Q&A functionality and real-time updates for answers/documents uploaded – An auction platform (English auction with binding public bids) with the ability to solicit nonbinding bids (market soundings), set reserve prices, etc.
Data review and validation	Automated checks to provide a level of assurance on data quality/ analytics	• In order to reduce transaction and search costs, the NPL platform would ensure data sharing and a high degree of data standardization. Completeness and other checks could be built in to enhance data quality as well as a range of data analytics tools. • Unlikely to fully remove the need for additional due diligence, but fundamental to success.
Data warehousing	Hosting of detailed loan portfolio information (financial and nonfinancial data)	• Electronic (virtual) data room, regularly updated with detailed loan-level data, including both financial information and other qualitative information (e.g., legal documentation, security documents, payment history, collateral appraisals, borrower correspondence, etc.).
Ancillary services	Intermediation for other value accretive services	• Credit servicing (including in terms of data provision) • Valuation and due diligence • Real estate and collateral appraisal

Portfolios visible to more potential investors and greater transparency

Reduced bid-ask spread, higher prices, faster resolution

NDA = nondisclosure agreement, NPL = nonperforming loan, Q&A = question and answer.
Source: Asian Development Bank. 2022. Road Map for Developing an Online Platform to Trade Nonperforming Loans in Asia and the Pacific. Manila. https://www.adb.org/publications/road-map-online-platform-trade-nonperforming-loans.

The platform's core services facilitate transactions through connecting buyers and sellers and running auctions (see Figure 1, **transaction facilitation**). Platforms provide data services as part of their core offering or as additional value-added services. Data services include data preparation, review, and validation including the creation, transformation, and automated checking of standardized data templates (**data preparation services**). Platform services can include a data warehouse or data hub service where transaction data are collected in a central repository to support platform users with the ongoing monitoring of transaction and performance data, regulatory reporting requirements, and access to benchmark data for trade comparable and better pricing (**data hub services**). Platforms can offer a multitude of additional ancillary services like valuation tools or virtual data rooms and due diligence support tools (**valuation and due diligence support**). Platforms can offer self-service online software or fully managed execution advisory services (**advisory services**). Platforms can provide standardized legal documents or accept the use of transaction documents proposed by the seller and subject to negotiation by the buyer. Platforms can provide information only or facilitate payment and settlement of the assets (**payment and settlement**). Existing platforms can be used by sellers who place their assets on the platform. Existing platforms can also be insourced as white-labelled software solutions operating under the name and logo of the seller.

Specific regulation that governs the establishment and running of NPL transaction platforms does not exist in any country. Kazakhstan is implementing an accreditation process for NPL trading platforms.

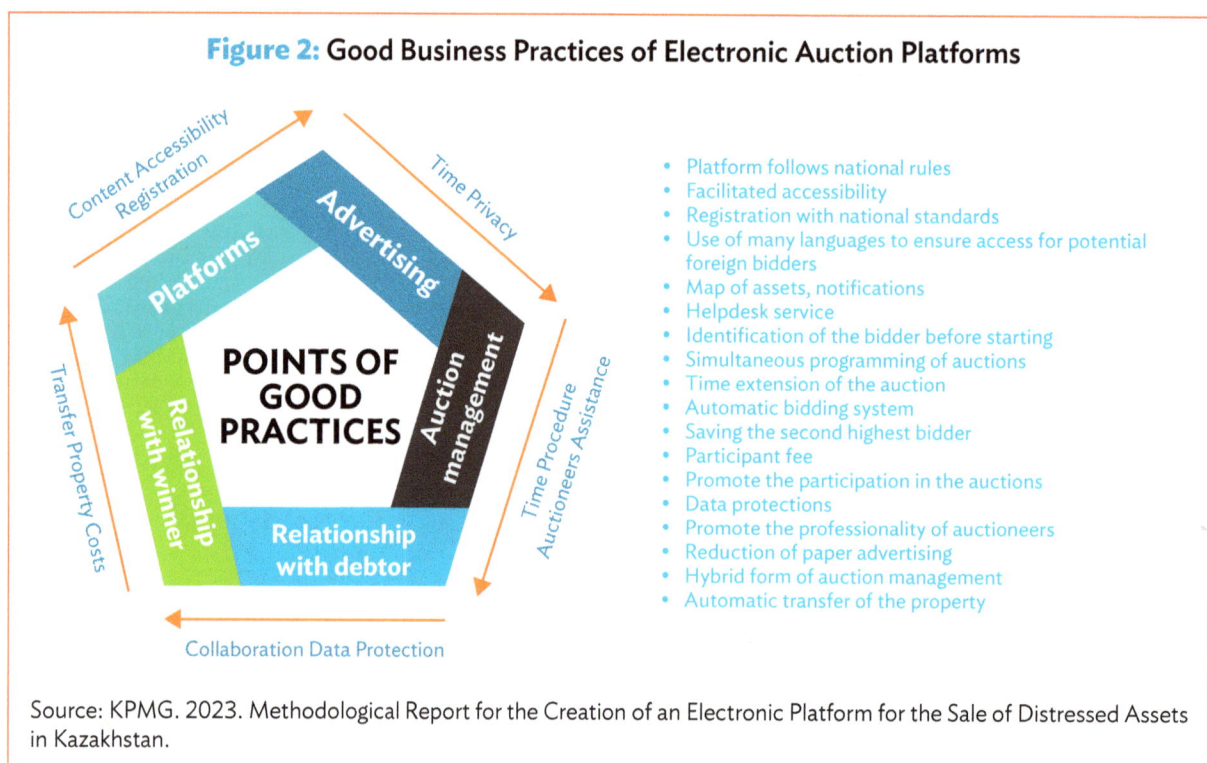

Figure 2: Good Business Practices of Electronic Auction Platforms

POINTS OF GOOD PRACTICES

- Platform follows national rules
- Facilitated accessibility
- Registration with national standards
- Use of many languages to ensure access for potential foreign bidders
- Map of assets, notifications
- Helpdesk service
- Identification of the bidder before starting
- Simultaneous programming of auctions
- Time extension of the auction
- Automatic bidding system
- Saving the second highest bidder
- Participant fee
- Promote the participation in the auctions
- Data protections
- Promote the professionality of auctioneers
- Reduction of paper advertising
- Hybrid form of auction management
- Automatic transfer of the property

Source: KPMG. 2023. Methodological Report for the Creation of an Electronic Platform for the Sale of Distressed Assets in Kazakhstan.

Good practices: NPL transaction platforms should support good business practices and comply with national legal and regulatory standards and market conventions (Figure 2).[2] Platforms should support the full sequence of main activities necessary to achieve a successful outcome as part of a competitive transaction process. Platforms should support the specific stages to be followed throughout a sale. Highlighted key activities and deliverables for each phase include the following:

■ Transaction structuring and asset selection to determine the optimal perimeter for the seller. For instance, the targeted investor base may not be interested in certain assets which should then be removed from the transaction portfolio for a better auction result.

■ Preparation phase concerning data tape, teaser, nondisclosure agreements, and process letters, or VDR for due diligence as required.

---

[2]   Figure 2 draws on draft guidelines from the Council of Europe's European Commission for the Efficiency of Justice on judicial e-auctions.

- The bidding process itself with distribution of the asset information pack, possible selection of major auction types, and selection of winner.
- Signing of the transaction transfer documents and financial closing.
- Ancillary pre- and post-auction activities like borrower notifications.

General principles for nonperforming loan trading platforms: Platforms should meet several principles, whether operated by private third-parties or sponsored by government agencies:

Accessibility for sellers and buyers and compliance with legislative and regulatory requirements: All eligible buyers should be entitled to purchase distressed assets via the platform and the platform should clearly state any requirements on eligibility to participate in the sales process. The platform operator will also ensure that (i) only eligible buyers take part in auctions related to certain types of NPLs, and (ii) buyers are notified about any additional legal or financial requirements ahead of the auction.

Transparency: Platform operators must ensure provision of information in accordance with approved templates and guarantee auctions are conducted in accordance with established rules.

Data integrity: Data standardization and consistency based on public data templates on the platform will reduce information asymmetries between potential investors and sellers. Operators may also conduct basic data validation and provide value-added services for prospective investors.

Security: Technical maturity and high-level cybersecurity. Operators should ensure efficient security tools are incorporated into the platform to ensure no impact on auction results or unauthorized access to data.

Support for key execution steps within the overall asset purchase process and simulation of each step from perspective of sellers and buyers. The steps (detailed in Chapter 5) include the following:

(i) **User registration:** Platform user (sellers and buyers) registration on the platform. Acknowledgment of key platform terms and conditions, data processing agreements and additional know-your-customer (KYC) requirements like compliance with international sanctions or anti-money laundering (AML) rules.

(ii) **Data preparation:** Preparation of a transaction summary (teaser) and posting data about the assets for sale on the platform. Creation of a standardized data tape.

(iii) **Nondisclosure agreement, process letter, and optional nonbinding offer:** Signing of asset-specific nondisclosure agreements and process letters. Optional use of a nonbinding offer phase to preselect suitable buyers for the auction of complex assets.

(iv) **Virtual data room and due diligence:** Access to a VDR to access unstructured data supplementing the loan data tape.

(v) **Auction execution:** Prepare specific auction terms and parameters, advertise auction terms, or directly invite potential buyers to participate in the auction. Support the negotiation of sales and purchase agreements and (electronically) sign them. Inform bidders, and record, archive, and publish auction outcomes. Optionally, provide post-auction support with borrower notifications and support document transfers to the winning bidder.

(vi) **Communication tools, help desk, and complaints procedure:** Offer online communication tools to allow investors to ask questions at any time or as specified in the auction process. Provide technical help desk support to all users accessing the platform. Have clearly defined complaints procedures.

2 Nonperforming Loan Trading Platforms in Asia and the Pacific and Beyond

The Asian NPL market is dominated by the PRC in volume and number of transactions. Deloitte estimates $707 billion of NPLs in Asia and the Pacific at the end of 2022, of which the PRC holds $432 billion followed by Japan ($104 billion) (Deloitte 2023). Annual NPL trades over the last few years exceeded $100 billion in the PRC, among the largest NPL markets globally and larger than all other Asian NPL markets combined.

Extensive monetary and fiscal measures enabled Asian banks to rebound from the pandemic with robust revenue growth from higher margins, lower than expected credit losses and higher capital ratios. However, NPLs are expected to rise in the medium term due to a combination of factors, including declining property values in some economies, increasing corporate insolvencies, higher interest rates, and the inability of certain borrowers to refinance due to evolving bank risk tolerance. Against this backdrop, ADB has expressed interest in online NPL trading platforms to develop the Asian NPL market and manage growing NPL volumes more efficiently.

2.1 Nonperforming Loan Trading and Platform Use in Selected Countries

In the US and Europe, dedicated NPL trading platforms have operated for years as private sector companies. Multiple platforms compete with traditional transaction advisors offering bespoke transaction services and ancillary functions like data preparation, valuation, and data warehousing. The share of online platforms in overall NPL trading volumes is unknown, but it is still believed to be small in many countries where platform operations are relatively recent. For example, DebtX has operated in the US for more than 20 years, whereas platforms established more recently in Europe, such as Debitos or NPL Markets, are active in many countries, including Italy and Greece, the two largest European markets for NPLs.

2.1.1 People's Republic of China

In the PRC, the International Monetary Fund's October 2023 World Economic Outlook (IMF 2023) expects subdued core inflation below 2% amid substantial economic slack, with rising youth unemployment and pass-through from lower energy costs. The real gross domestic product (GDP) grew by 5.2% in 2023 and ADB projects GDP growth of 4.5% in 2024.[3] And in the third quarter of 2023, the NPL ratio of commercial banks in the PRC was 1.62%, or CNY3.2 trillion ($448 billion) (Figure 3).

---

[3] ADB Data Library. https://data.adb.org/dataset/gdp-growth-asia-and-pacific-asian-development-outlook.

Figure 3: **Nonperforming Loan Ratio in the People's Republic of China**

NPL ratio

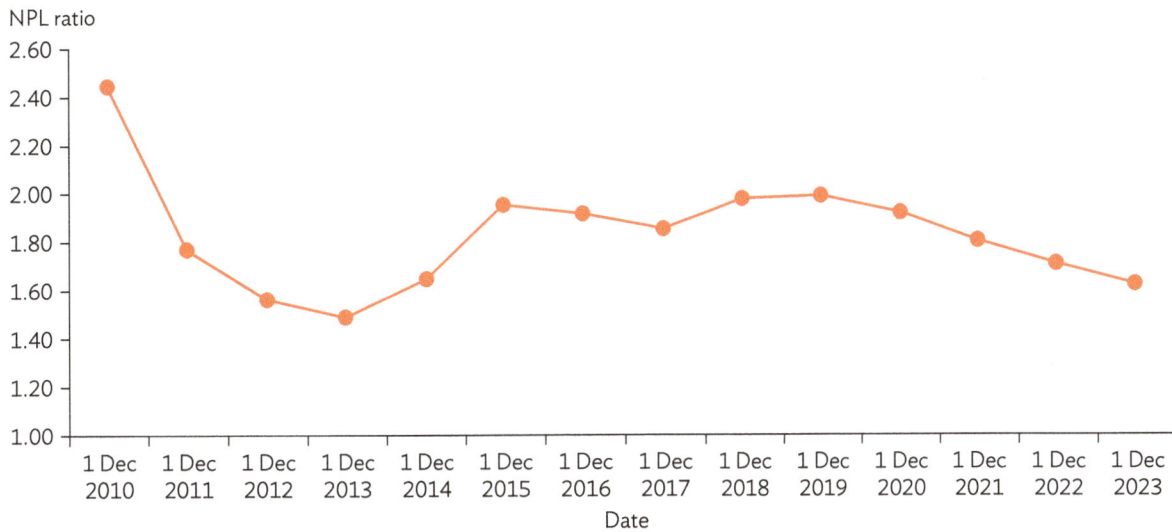

Date

NPL = nonperforming loan.
Source: CEIC Data. www.ceicdata.com (accessed 19 April 2024).

Among economic issues in 2023, respondents to the ADB IPAF survey from public AMCs in the PRC identified the three most pressing concerns as falling real estate prices, slow economic growth, and high unemployment. The country's stock of NPLs is expected to increase slightly over the next 2 years with a new wave of NPL formation expected to peak in 2024. All sectors are likely to experience higher NPL levels. Strategic tools frequently used in the PRC for resolving NPL issues include NPL write-off, debt restructuring, legal enforcement procedures, direct NPL portfolio sale to investors, public and private AMCs, and NPL securitization. The current state of the NPL market in the country is described as having a sizeable and active NPL market with secondary transactions. All major asset classes including commercial real estate, residential real estate, secured corporate or small and medium-sized enterprises (SMEs) lending, unsecured corporate or SME lending, and retail loans are actively traded in the market for NPLs. Interest exists in having a central data hub for NPL transaction data and historical performance data in the country.

Online auction platforms are used extensively for the public sale of foreclosed properties and other items sold in judicial auctions. Online collateral auctions in the first half of 2023 totaled 221,000 for transaction volume of CNY79.3 billion ($11.1 billion). Residential real estate dominated judicial auctions, with 200,000 assets and volume of CNY61.6 billion ($8.6 billion). In the first 7 months of 2023, average discounts for online NPL transactions were 66.3% and average number of monthly NPL auctions on the Ali Auction platform was 3,400 (Zheshang Asset Research Institute 2023).[4]

Zheshang Asset Management Company is a large regional public AMC in the PRC operating across the entire country. It routinely uses any of the large private sector online platforms to sell assets while also operating and building their own online platform. This is the first online platform operated by any of the public AMCs in the PRC.

---

[4] Research from the Zheshang Asset Research Institute. ADB's discussions with ZSAMC's Chief Technology Officer.

Among the NPL disposal platforms in the PRC, independent third-party online auction platforms dominate the market, which publish information on assets and facilitate transactions. Some of them may have independent trading systems and settlement systems to ensure the stability and security of transactions. From the perspective of official authorization, the online platforms can broadly fall into two categories: online trading platforms designated by the Supreme Court, such as Taobao.com or JD.com; and other unofficial online platforms, such as 360pai.com.

Taobao.com/Ali Auction is an online auction platform founded by Alibaba Group in 2007, and that launched an independent mobile app in September 2021. It is the world's largest online auction market. Taobao has cooperated with thousands of commercial institutions, government agencies, and financial institutions. The main business segments of Taobao include high-priced asset auctions, luxury goods auctions, and collections auctions. It operates mainly a business-to-consumer (B2C) business model, with 5 million daily domestic users, and conducted more than 560,000 judicial auction cases in 2021.[5] The data from auction results are used to value NPLs, which are mostly loans secured by residential real estate. The use of public auctions is mandatory for AMCs to sell assets, the sale price of a successful auction is disclosed, but not the identity of the buyer. Sellers are responsible for the information uploaded to the platform and the information is not verified by Taobao. Standard data templates are used. Most commercial banks use the platform for individual asset sales, but large portfolio trades may happen outside the platform. The participation rate of international investors is very low. Taobao plans to become more active with cross-border transactions in their 10-year plan.

Baichang Technology, established in 2018 and operating under the 360pai.com brand, is a significant player in the PRC's special asset industry. The state-owned company is backed by investment from Shanghai Minhang Asset Investment and Management (Group) Co., Ltd. and holds a legal auction operation license. 360pai's core services span financial asset trading, online auctions for state-owned asset leasing rights, disposal services, and digital technology solutions. Its clients include financial institutions, government enterprises, state-owned companies, asset management firms, and specialized investors. The company acts as an aggregator and offers services to over 500 auction companies. The company works with standardized data templates and offers offline professional support services around data and execution. NPL transactions take 2 to 3 months to complete and longer for the most complex deals.[6]

2.1.2 Republic of Korea

In the Republic of Korea in mid-year 2023, domestic banks carried NPLs at 0.41%, or $80.86 billion out of $1.97 trillion in total loans, explaining a lack of NPL transactions in this country due to relatively low stocks (Figure 4). In 2022, Deloitte reported total size of NPL transactions as W2.4 trillion ($1.8 billion) (Deloitte 2023). The average NPL sales price as a percentage of outstanding principal balance increased to 79.6%. The NPL market is expected to double in the next 2 years to reach W5 trillion ($3.9 billion) because of challenges in the real estate market and rising interest rates. COVID-19 forbearance measures were extended in 2023 and will now expire in March 2024. Recently, the nonperforming ratio of credit card loans has increased to 1.27% and several digital banks and nonbank lenders show NPL ratios above 3%.

---

[5]   Zheshang Asset Research Institute. *Success Factors and Case Studies of Online Platforms in the People's Republic of China.*
[6]   ADB's discussions with 360pai officials on 5 July 2023.

Figure 4: **Nonperforming Loan Ratio in the Republic of Korea**

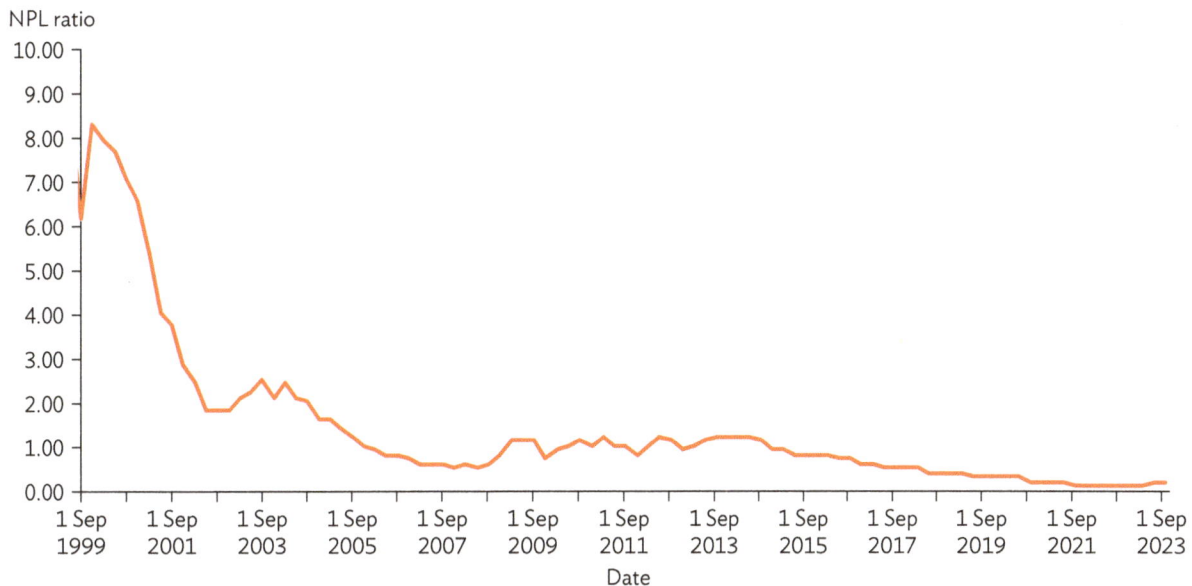

NPL = nonperforming loan.
Source: CEIC. Financial Supervisory Service. www.ceicdata.com (accessed 19 April 2024).

Overall, the NPL market is mature, with portfolios marketed across a wide range of asset classes, including commercial and residential mortgages, corporate loans, and shipping finance. The four largest buyers (UAMCO, Hana, Daishin, and Woori) represented 92% of the market. Private AMCs such as UAMCO and Daishin operate differently from public entities like KAMCO. There is no significant demand for NPLs from foreign investors in the market of the Republic of Korea. The government's ban on financial institutions selling consumer NPLs since 2021 as a temporary COVID-19 protection measure has reduced the size of the market, whereas sales to KAMCO are still possible.

Recovery rates in the Republic of Korea vary based on the nature of the debt. For secured debts, the recovery rate depends on collateral values, reaching nearly 100% for residential mortgages in a good real estate market. The recovery period for secured debt is 8 to 12 months, while unsecured debt collections follow the remaining statute of limitations, which can be extended indefinitely for large claim amounts.

KAMCO has established a strong presence in the asset trading domain through its tailored online platform, OnBid, launched in 2002. The platform is a dedicated channel for the sale of state-owned, foreclosed, or entrusted properties managed by KAMCO and other public sector assets (Figure 5). KAMCO's OnBid asset sales predominantly comprise real estate, land, and various non-movable and movable assets. Foreign participation in OnBid's asset purchases remains limited, accounting for less than 10% of total sales. Individual assets form the core of OnBid's transactions, with portfolio sales representing a minor portion of their sales strategy.

KAMCO conducts comprehensive asset valuations prior to initiating the sales process, employing these valuations as the initial transaction prices. Auction methodologies, including English and Dutch methods, are employed for asset sales, and outcomes are publicly disclosed through both the platform and media channels.

By offering standardized legal templates and facilitating online due diligence, KAMCO streamlines the asset acquisition process for investors. Beyond its primary activities, KAMCO also extends brokerage services to other public entities. Cumulative transaction volumes of OnBid since inception exceeded $100 billion in 2022, with 20,000 sellers and 2.5 million bid participants. Of assets sold on OnBid, 53% were real estate-related, 22% vehicles and machinery, and 25% goods and other assets.

For complex assets, an accounting firm provides an appraisal and buyers and sellers organize roll-up meetings to avoid any misinterpretation of the information provided. Contrary to many judicial auctions in other countries, buyers on OnBid can contact the seller and arrange on-site inspections prior to bidding on real estate and can get bank financing. For judicial auctions, the court discloses winning bid information and specialist data providers in the Republic of Korea, such as Infocare, collect the information for collateral valuations. All lawsuit contents can be viewed and cross-verified on the Supreme Court's My Case inquiry.

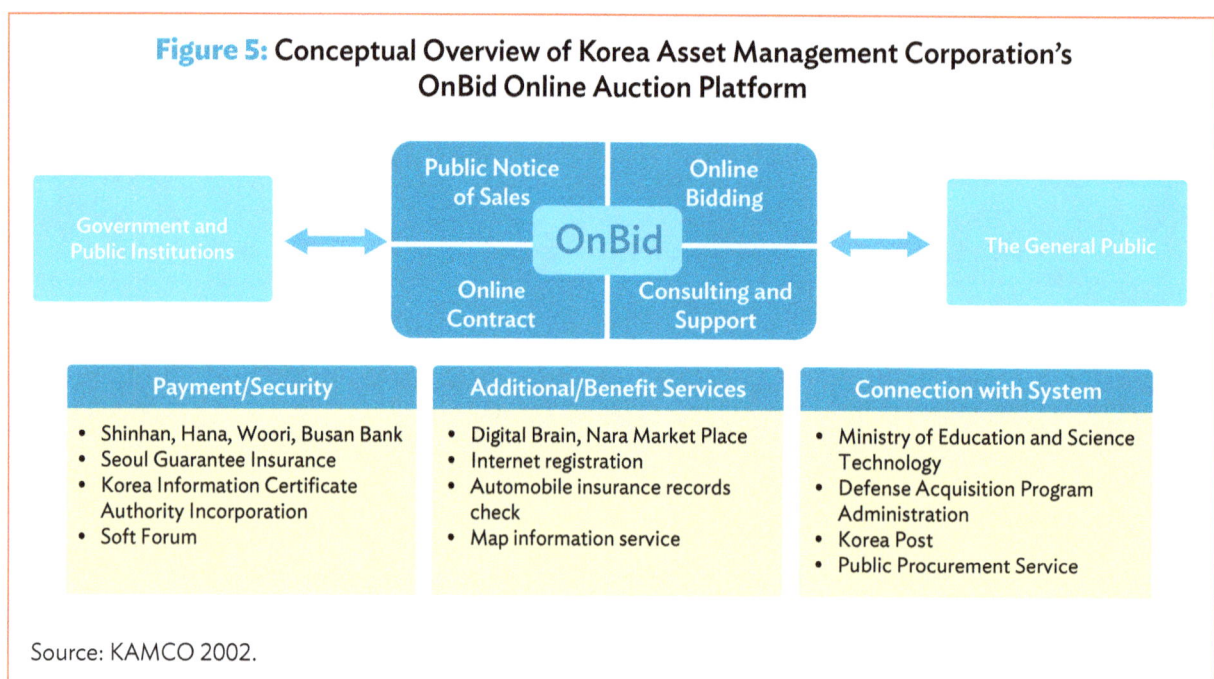

Figure 5: Conceptual Overview of Korea Asset Management Corporation's OnBid Online Auction Platform

Source: KAMCO 2002.

2.1.3 Kazakhstan

At the beginning of 2022, the President of Kazakhstan ordered the government to create a digital platform for distressed assets sales, and introduced incentives to prompt market players to trade NPLs more actively. Total NPLs in Kazakhstan are relatively low, at less than $2 billion, and the NPL ratio in August 2023 was reported at 3.4% (Figure 6 shows the NPL ratio from mid-July 2018 through the start of 2023). To date, the public AMC of Kazakhstan, the Fund of Problem Loans, uses its own website to announce NPL sales, whereas it uses an electronic auction platform for property sales.

The Fund of Problem Loans conducted a feasibility study in 2022 in cooperation with the European Bank for Reconstruction and Development and KPMG to determine the most appropriate model for further digitalization of NPL sales in Kazakhstan, covering governance and operational issues, including a cost estimates implementation timeframe.

Figure 6: Nonperforming Loan Ratio in Kazakhstan

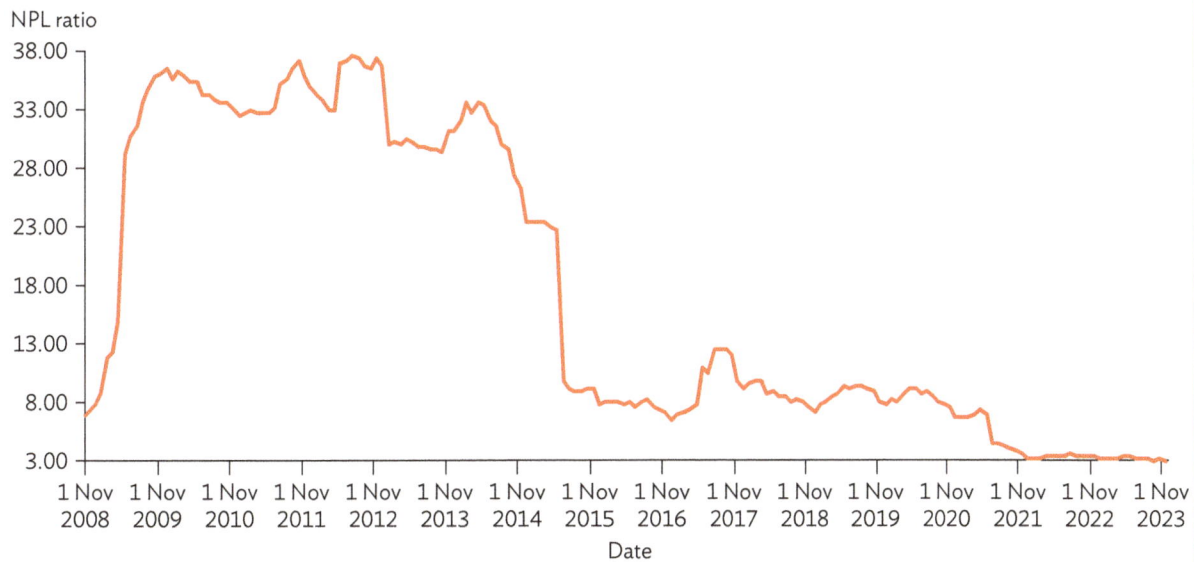

NPL = nonperforming loan.
Source: CEIC Data. National Bank of Kazakhstan (accessed 19 April 2024).

The feasibility study aimed mainly to evaluate the need to create a single national platform for NPL sales. However, the main conclusion was that it would be more appropriate for Kazakhstan financial regulators to create conditions that would encourage existing and potential market players to develop or upgrade electronic platforms for the sale of assets to meet requirements in functionality, security, and transparency. The feasibility study recommended the following steps, which are currently in the legal implementation process (KPMG 2023):

■ Oblige commercial banks and other holders of distressed assets to sell such assets exclusively via accredited electronic platforms.

■ Introduce an accreditation process, led by the financial market regulator. Non-accredited platforms will continue to exist as marketplaces, offering assets for sale but prohibited from conducting auctions.

■ Restrict the nontransparent process of NPL transfers from commercial banks to their individual AMCs by requiring preparation of a valuation report.

■ Introduce data templates for NPL and foreclosed asset sales, which is part of the accreditation process.

While the new regulation for the use of platform and standardized templates should increase transparency, a concern remains that NPL transfers from banks to affiliated AMCs may continue to happen at transfer prices that do not reflect the open market value of the assets. Interestingly, the Kazakh feasibility study also considers a platform-of-platforms model, i.e., a central, publicly owned platform that acts as a data exchange but would also provide auction-related services. While the case is strong for increased transparency through standardized data templates and the mandatory use of a central data hub, there is no compelling reason to centralize the auction function, and this model is not currently pursued in Kazakhstan.

2.1.4 Thailand

According to the Bank of Thailand, the banking system's loans contracted a marginal 0.4% year-on-year in the second quarter of 2023, due to the gradual repayment of businesses loans, particularly from SMEs. Bank lending continued to expand mainly in large corporate loans, mortgage loans, and personal loans. Loan quality deteriorated slightly in SMEs and among consumer loans. The banking system's gross nonperforming loans (NPL or stage 3) declined to B492.3 billion ($13.8 billion), equivalent to an NPL ratio of 2.67%. Meanwhile, the ratio of loans with a significant increase in credit risk (stage 2) stood at 6.08%. As in other countries in the region, the Thai financial sector is undergoing a digital transformation, with many financial institutions shifting their business models and utilizing data and technology to create new products and services for customers. However, the use of NPL transaction platforms is still uncommon.

According to a survey conducted by ADB among public AMCs in Asia and the Pacific (IPAF members),[7] Thailand faces modestly increasing NPLs through 2025 due to economic headwinds. Sellers of NPLs in Thailand benefit from more than 100 public and private AMCs competing for NPL sales. Commercial real estate and residential real estate loans are the most typical NPLs traded. While Thailand is considered to have a relatively high readiness for NPL trading, some barriers to NPL resolution exist, including underdeveloped capital and money markets, an immature legal framework around enforcement processes, and legal/regulatory restrictions on NPL disposals.

Thailand does not see the need for an online NPL trading platform due to the underdeveloped legal and regulatory regimes around NPL disposal and concerns about data protection, data quality, and the general complexity of establishing and operating such a platform in the country. According to survey responses, invoices/accounts receivable and securities (e.g., stocks, bonds) are considered the most suitable collateral types for online NPL trading in Thailand. The country's securitization regime permits NPLs to be used as underlying assets for securitization, but there have been no observed instances of NPL securitization activity.

The loan servicing industry in Thailand, both for secured and unsecured loans, is described as somewhat active, comprising several domestic players. However, operational improvements, including personnel and IT development, are needed to enhance its effectiveness. Enforcing a defaulted unsecured consumer loan in the courts in Thailand typically takes 6 to 12 months, whereas enforcing a defaulted residential mortgage loan in the courts in Thailand typically takes about 12 months. The survey responses from Thailand welcomed the idea of a central data hub for NPL transaction data and historical performance data. Such a hub would facilitate the collection and sharing of information related to NPL transactions, potentially enhancing transparency and market efficiency in this context.

2.1.5 Viet Nam

Viet Nam is one of the few countries where inflation in 2023 averaged below its target rate (of 4.5% and at 3.25%) according to the General Statistics Office (other such countries include the PRC and Thailand). Subdued core inflation reflected a slowdown in economic activity and pass-through from lower energy prices.

---

[7]   Republic of Korea: Korea Asset Management Corp., Korea Deposit Insurance Corp. Thailand: Sukhumvit Asset Management Co., Ltd., Deposit Protection Agency. PRC: China Cinda Asset Mgt. Co., Ltd.; China Great Wall Asset Management Co. Ltd, China Huarong Asset Management Co. Ltd., Orient Asset Management Co. Ltd., Zheshang Asset Management Co. Ltd. Viet Nam: Debt and Asset Trading Corp., Vietnam Asset Management Co., Kazakhstan: Fund of Problem Loans. Mongolia: Mongolian Asset Management Corp., Deposit insurance corporations. Malaysia: Perbadanan Insurans Deposit Malaysia, Agensi Kaunseling dan Pengurusan Kredit. Indonesia: PT Perusahaan Pengelola Aset (Persero).

According to ADB, Viet Nam's real GDP grew a very healthy 8% in 2022 and at 5.05% in 2023 and is expected to increase to 6.0% in 2024. The unemployment rate among the working age population stood at 2.28% in 2023 and is expected to remain low at 2.1% in 2024 (2.3% in 2022). The global economic situation, which has fluctuated, has negatively impacted the domestic business operations and reduced the ability of some customers to repay principal and interest to banks.

Despite a robust economy, tensions in the real estate market have led to an increase in NPLs. As can be seen in Figure 7, the NPL ratio doubled to 4.93% in the year to September 2023. Banks' NPL coverage ratios recently declined but are still at or above 100% (Figure 8).

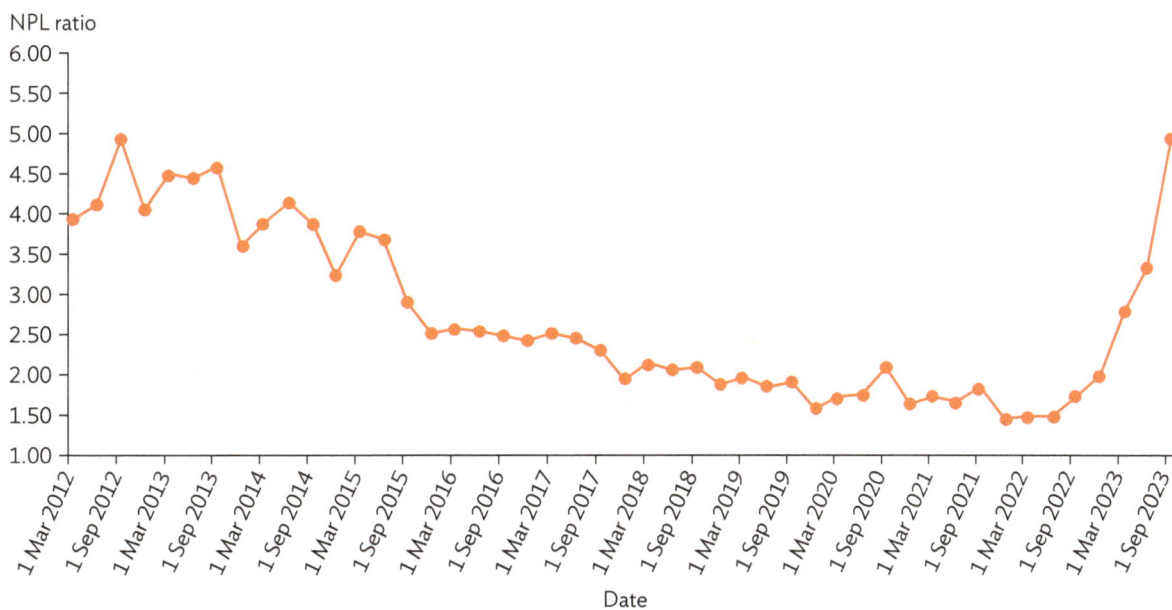

Figure 7: Nonperforming Loan Ratio in Viet Nam

NPL = nonperforming loan.
Source: State Bank of Vietnam, CEIC (accessed 19 April 2024).

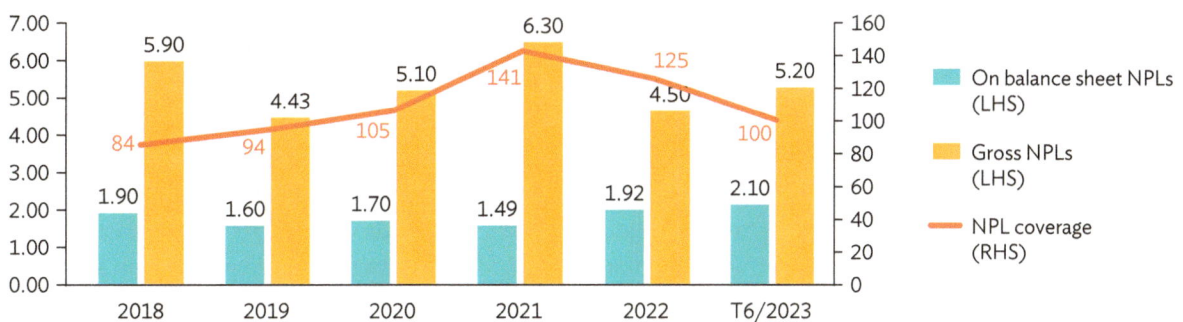

Figure 8: Nonperforming Loan Ratios and Nonperforming Loan Coverage Ratios of Vietnamese Banks

LHS = left-hand side, NPL = nonperforming loan, RHS = right-hand side.
Sources: BIDV Research, State Bank of Vietnam, and banks' financial statements.

Respondents to the ADB IPAF survey expected that NPLs in Viet Nam would peak in 2024. All sectors are likely to experience higher NPLs, including corporate/SMEs lending, commercial real estate, residential real estate, and unsecured personal loans. Public AMCs are identified as the top NPL buyers in Viet Nam. Debt trading in Viet Nam is mainly carried out via contracts, while in other countries, such as the Republic of Korea or Italy, debts are converted into marketable securities through securitization.

The availability of an NPL trading platform would make it easier for investors to access official and credible information on certain debts, which would promote transactions of bad debts. The VAMC-Loan Transaction Platform Branch is the first debt trading platform dedicated to Viet Nam and started operations, as noted, in 2021. The transaction platform provides consultation and brokerage services in trading debts of individuals and corporations and serves as an intermediary in arranging such transactions between third parties. VAMC's intention behind the setup of the platform is to provide a new, effective, and professional service in resolving bad debts, in turn promoting the development of the debt market with the agency playing a key role in facilitating debt trading activities.

The establishment of VAMC-Loan Transaction Platform Branch was seen as an important and positive contribution to Viet Nam's debt trading activities and will help accelerate the debt recovery process (SBV 2022). The State Bank of Vietnam (SBV) assessed that Viet Nam's debt trading market was still in its early stages, and there are several issues that need to be addressed, for instance, the inconsistent and inadequate legal framework for debt trading or limitations of the IT and data infrastructure. Based on the signed master agreements and debt trading contracts, the transaction platform has posted information and listed the debt and collateral of the debt on the website with a total value of outstanding loans of D38,000 billion ($1.6 billion). Successfully executed consulting contracts with customers reached nearly D450 billion ($18 million). The transaction platform is continuing to prepare brokerage and consulting contracts with customers.

It is also continuing to improve its operating mechanism with new features to facilitate more convenient interaction with credit institutions and the use of self-updating as well as self-publishing information on debt sale, collateral asset sale, and at the same time creating favorable conditions for investors in accessing information from credit institutions. The operation of the transaction platform still faces difficulties and challenges, especially in attracting new customers to participate in transactions on the platform.

2.1.6 World Bank Study on Public Asset Management Company Use of Nonperforming Loan Trading Platforms

Working closely with the VAMC in 2022, the World Bank prepared a comprehensive survey for AMCs to explore the main aspects of electronic debt trading platforms (World Bank 2022). The survey comprised 44 questions related to 4 key areas of interest to the VAMC: (i) general information about platforms, (ii) the preparatory phase for trading, (iii) the sale process, and (iv) additional services offered to investors. The survey was sent to 12 potential participants in Asia and the Pacific and Europe, and of 8 respondents, only 2 actively used the platform. Potential participants, all with extensive track records of managing and selling distressed loans and/or foreclosed assets, were eight operational public AMCs, three deposit insurance agencies, and KAMCO, whose mandate includes the sale of state assets. Of the eight survey responses in 2022,[8] only two, KAMCO and the Ukraine Deposit Guarantee Fund, actively used an electronic

---

[8]   A presentation by Li Chuanquan, executive deputy general manager, chief strategy officer, Zhejiang Zheshang Asset Management Co. Ltd. at the International Public Asset Management Company Forum in 2022 reported widespread use of third-party auction platforms by AMCs to sell loans, although none of the PRC AMCs responded to the survey.

debt trading platform. Five respondents, Thai Sukhumvit Asset Management, Philippine Deposit Insurance Corporation, National Asset Management Agency of Ireland, the Spanish Management Company for Assets arising from the Restructuring of the Banking Sector (Sareb), and Bank Assets Management Company of Slovenia, reported limited use of the internet in the sales process. And one, the Deposit Insurance Corporation of Japan, reported no use of the internet to sell assets.

Development of an electronic debt trading platform can be costly and time-consuming. KAMCO reported the system took about 20 experts 18 months to develop at an initial cost of $2 million. Market price is discovered during the auction process and published in media and on the platforms themselves. Both KAMCO and Ukraine Deposit Guarantee Fund utilize English auction methodology, and both allow multiple auctions for a given asset. Ukraine Deposit Guarantee Fund allows the price to be reduced by 10% of the initial starting price in subsequent rounds up to a maximum of 30%. If the asset fails to sell at this point, it is placed for sale in a Dutch auction. If it still fails to sell, assets are pooled with others and sold as a portfolio in a Dutch auction. Any remaining assets at this stage are pooled by the originating bank and sold as one pool.

KAMCO and the Ukraine Deposit Guarantee Fund publish the results of all sales transacted on their platforms. Both platforms provide a wide range of information to investors and use standardized legal templates to settle transactions. Both organizations also actively have market assets to achieve better results.

2.2 Pros and Cons of Nonperforming Loan Trading Platforms

Table 1 compares the main functions of online auction and NPL trading platforms in Asia and the Pacific with some international platforms. Platforms vary by user type, asset type, and ancillary function, including valuation services and data hub functions.

Table 1: Overview of Selected Asian and International Nonperforming Loan Trading Platforms

Asian Platforms	Debt Exchange	OnBid	360pal	Taobao
Regional activity	Asia Domestic	Asia Domestic	Asia Domestic	Asia Domestic
Country of establishment	Viet Nam	Republic of Korea	PRC	PRC
Main countries	Viet Nam	Republic of Korea	PRC	PRC
Public AMC sponsored	VAMC	KAMCO	N	N
Main asset classes	Corporate NPL and REO	REO	REO and NPL	REO and NPL
Main investor type	AMC and Institutional	Private	Institutional	Private
Auction platform	Y	Y	Y	Y
Judicial auctions	N	N	N	Y
Sale of own assets	Y (VAMC)	Y (KAMCO)	N	N
Transaction advisory	Y	Y	Y	N
Virtual data room service	N	Y	Y	Y

continued on next page

Table 1 *continued*

Asian Platforms	Debt Exchange	OnBid	360pal	Taobao
Valuation advisory	N	N	Y	Y
Data hub and reporting	N	N	N	N
Data enrichment and validation	N	Y	Y	N

Other Platforms	ProZorro.Sale	NPL Markets	Debitos	DebtX
Regional activity	Europe Domestic	Europe and international	Europe and international	US and international
Country of establishment	Ukraine	UK	Germany	US
Main countries	Ukraine	Italy, UK, Spain, Greece, Mexico	Germany, Italy, Greece	US
Public AMC sponsored	Deposit Guarantee Fund	N	N	N
Main asset classes	Corporate NPL and REO	Retail NPL, Corporate NPL, REO	Retail NPL, Corporate NPL, REO	Real Estate PL and NPL
Main investor type	Institutional	Institutional	Institutional	Institutional
Auction platform	Y	Y	Y	Y
Judicial auctions	N	N	N	N
Sale of own assets	Y (DGF)	N	N	N
Transaction advisory	N	Y	Y	Y
Virtual data room service	N	Y	Y	Y
Valuation advisory	N	Y	N	Y
Data hub and reporting	N	Y	N	N
Data enrichment and validation	N	Y	N	Y

AMC = asset management company, DGF = deposit guarantee fund, KAMCO = Korea Asset Management Corporation, N = no, NPL = nonperforming loan, PL = performing loan, PRC = People's Republic of China, REO = real estate owned, UK = United Kingdom, US = United States, VAMC = Vietnam Asset Management Company, Y = yes.
Source: Authors.

The effective operations of an NPL trading platform hinge on robust infrastructure that can only thrive with a conducive environment promoting investment. A platform is a tool to facilitate the sale of loans or tangible assets. It does not ensure that investors will be interested in purchasing assets. However, it can help convince investors that a well-developed supportive infrastructure is in place which will aid rather than hinder their ability to earn a profit. The success of online NPL sale platforms relies on a supportive framework, encompassing a robust creditor rights system ensuring equitable treatment, transparent mechanisms for open bidding and equal access to information for all potential investors, and a network of reputable third parties like lawyers, accountants, and asset servicers who can guide investors through resolution processes. Table 2 summarizes the pros and cons of NPL trading platforms.

Table 2: Pros and Cons of Online Nonperforming Loan Transaction Platforms

Pros	Cons
Information accessibility: NPL platforms enable comprehensive online displays of asset details, facilitating efficient communication and negotiation.	**Resource intensive:** Establishing and maintaining NPL platforms requires significant resources and operational efforts.
Transparent ecosystem: Integration of third-party service providers enhances transparency in asset disposal transactions.	**Transaction costs:** Using an independent NPL platform incurs transaction costs, which, however, tend to be below those of traditional brokers and transaction advisors.
Operational efficiencies: Reduction of transaction costs and improved communication channels boost overall operational efficiency and accelerate the NPL disposal cycle.	**Limited foreign investor interest:** Some platforms face challenges in attracting foreign investors, limiting market expansion.
Data hub function: Utilization of big data contributes to informed decision-making and aligns background information for investors.	**Offline challenges:** Despite online features, complex business cases of NPLs often necessitate offline communication for negotiation and due diligence.
Multifaceted advantages: NPL platforms bring forth advantages such as publicity, negotiation efficiency, and improved decision-making.	

NPL = nonperforming loan.
Source: Authors.

Establishing and maintaining NPL trading platforms can be resource intensive. Using an independent NPL trading platform incurs a transaction cost. Many banks and other sellers list their NPLs and collateral assets for sale on a website run by the seller under its own brand and label. If the seller's website also offered an auction function, then the website would be an own-brand NPL sales platform. Such a platform can be built internally or purchased from external vendors. Even for large banks or AMCs it can be more time and cost efficient to buy existing software, which can be "white labelled," i.e., operated under the name and logo of the seller.

User-friendly interfaces are critical, and so are ancillary services, and offline transaction support requires skilled personnel or qualified external partners. To augment transparency, external valuers are often employed and in some jurisdictions their use is mandatory. Despite domestic market expansion, the Asian platforms presented in this section have garnered limited foreign interest. Cooperating with existing external platforms can help attract additional investors, especially cross-border, and thereby foster price competition and enhance the sale process dynamics.

Internet-based NPL trading platforms bring multifaceted advantages to streamline the process of asset disposal. One significant aspect pertains to information accessibility and publicity, as these platforms enable comprehensive displays of NPL details online, creating efficient channels for communication and negotiation between potential buyers and sellers. Integrating various service providers into the digital realm further enriches the ecosystem, allowing third-party companies with specialized services to offer transparent support for asset disposal transactions, enhancing the comprehensiveness and transparency of the process.

The data hub function, i.e., use of big data, constitutes another pivotal facet, with the establishment of dedicated databases for NPL disposal processes. By applying cutting-edge technology, some platforms analyze asset transaction and disposal data, contributing to informed decision-making. Facilitating background information alignment, the platform furnishes investors with comprehensive insights into the historical and current state of NPL projects, enabling them to make well-informed investment choices.

Operational efficiencies are notably improved through the reduction of transaction costs, achieved by bridging the gap between buyers and sellers and enriching communication channels. This, in turn, significantly diminishes negotiation expenses and boosts overall communication efficiency, ultimately lowering the costs associated with NPL disposal and transactions. These online platforms optimize time management and expedite the NPL disposal cycle. This acceleration aligns with the adoption of streamlined policies for NPL disposal, reducing the prevalence of large-scale portfolio approaches. While large-scale disposals will continue to be required in certain situations like bank rescues, they may come with a bulk price discount due to limited investor capacity and not matching individual assets with the most suitable buyer. By curbing such practices, the platforms enhance the recovery rate of NPLs, fostering a more effective and controlled disposition landscape.

However, some challenges remain due to the intricate nature of NPLs. While aspects such as searching for the most suitable target buyers and the actual bidding are undertaken online, the complex business cases tied to NPLs often necessitate offline communication for negotiation, due diligence, and price discussions. The challenge is to harmonize these two dimensions seamlessly.

2.3 Built-versus-Buy Considerations in Setting Up a Nonperforming Loan Trading Platform

A crucial consideration in establishing an online trading platform is whether to develop an internal platform or use an existing external one. The following aspects should be compared:[9]

Internal platform pros:

■ Suitable for strategic long-term operations with no sunset clauses.

■ Ideal for handling large-scale operations and the solution can grow with the deal volume.

■ Well suited for countries with specific legal and regulatory frameworks that are difficult to adopt by external platforms.

Internal platform cons:

■ Time-consuming and costly to establish initially, making it justifiable only for sellers and AMCs with long-term mandates and large-scale operations.

■ Will take significant time to establish, test, and launch. Most likely the initial launch will take 9 to 18 months, depending on the completeness of the initial services offered.

---

[9]   World Bank (2022) discusses the built-versus-buy decision.

- Breakeven cost analysis is required to justify the cost of creation. The cost of building an internal platform depends on the exact specification but will likely cost >$1 million for an initial version with limited ancillary features and services and cost could be significantly larger when including complex data warehouses, valuation tools, and VDR functions. Market utilities like the European Data Warehouse were initially built by external technology consultants at the cost of several million US dollars.

Internal platform challenges:

- Requires time and substantial marketing cost to attract investors and make them familiar with new interfaces, legal systems, and trading rules. Most sellers will have an existing database of investors, but capturing all relevant market players may require significant time and expense.
- Might be difficult to find the expertise to build a new platform in a specific country.

External platform pros:

- There are mature platforms in the market with a comprehensive product offering and operational experience, eliminating the need to create one from scratch.
- No initial time is required for establishment as the platforms are ready-to-use. Adopting existing platforms to a new jurisdiction will take some time, but typically no more than a few months.
- Provides access to an established diverse investor base familiar with the platforms interface, data rooms, and data and legal templates.
- Using external platforms for small-scale operations and occasional transactions is more cost efficient than setting up a dedicated corporate entity and building bespoke software. Platform fees vary and depend on the asset class, transaction size, and required service package, but can be less than $10,000 for a small NPL portfolio sale to institutional investors.[10]
- External platforms offer access to expertise concentrated in large global financial centers.

External platform cons:

- Platform fees for extended use periods of asset sale and large sales volumes might exceed the cost of creating and operating an internal platform in the long term. Note, however, that some platforms' providers offer their platform software tools and infrastructure on a subscription basis under a software-as-a-service (SaaS) business model which includes a white-labelled online presence. White labelling means that the software can be adjusted such that it shows the name, logo, colors, and text fonts of seller. Annual SaaS fees depend on the need for bespoke features, language and security requirements, bespoke transaction templates etc. but can be less than $50,000 a year for an off-the-shelf software service plus an initial set up fee.[11]
- External providers might offer an incomplete product or service for the seller and may lack detailed knowledge of the local market.

---

[10] B2C auction platforms have different fee structures and typically charge for each asset sold.

[11] Several independent debt trading platforms exist offering comprehensive services for debt sales (Chapter 1). The European platforms nplmarkets.com and debitos.com also offer white-labelled SaaS solutions.

3 Legal and Regulatory Framework for Nonperforming Loan Trading and Platforms

Recognizing that an effective NPL trading platform operates at the intricate intersection of financial systems and legal frameworks, this chapter addresses the core elements of an effective legal and regulatory framework for well-operating NPL trading platforms and markets. It examines the rules, guidelines, and oversight mechanisms currently in place, often drawing comparisons between existing systems and practices in the Republic of Korea and Viet Nam. The former's mature NPL market nonetheless does not use the existing online platform of KAMCO for NPL sales, while Viet Nam represents countries still developing legal and regulatory environments and have only recently established NPL platforms, operated by VAMC in the latter case. The two countries are used as case studies, given their current interest in online trading platforms and the active participation of KAMCO and VAMC in the IPAF cooperation with ADB.

To start, average recovery and NPL resolution times are compared in different countries that directly depend on the availability of out-of-court procedures and efficient judicial means to enforce collateral and resolve insolvencies.

3.1 International Benchmarks of Judicial and Nonperforming Loan Workout Efficiencies

- In jurisdictions with more efficient and modern insolvency frameworks, it takes less time to resolve cases and recovery rates are higher. Figure 9 shows time to recovery in years and recovery rates in cents on the dollar of outstanding claim for different countries according to the Doing Business database of the World Bank. Note that the Doing Business database was discontinued and an equivalent benchmark database with judicial efficiency measures has yet to be reestablished. In Singapore, Malaysia, the Republic of Korea, Thailand, and the PRC, completing the process takes from 0.8 to 1.7 years, below the average for Organisation for Economic Co-operation and Development (OECD) high-income jurisdictions.

Except for Solomon Islands and the PRC, recovery rates in this subgroup are above 50 cents per currency unit of the legal claim, with the highest rates in Singapore, at 89 cents per dollar.

According to the Doing Business 2020 survey, the East Asia and Pacific region is still heterogeneous in ease of resolving insolvencies, with the biggest economies and those that reformed their systems in the aftermath of the Asian financial crisis and the global financial crisis typically generally performing better.

Figure 9: **Time to Recovery in Years and Recovery Rate for Countries in Asia and the Pacific, Global Regions**

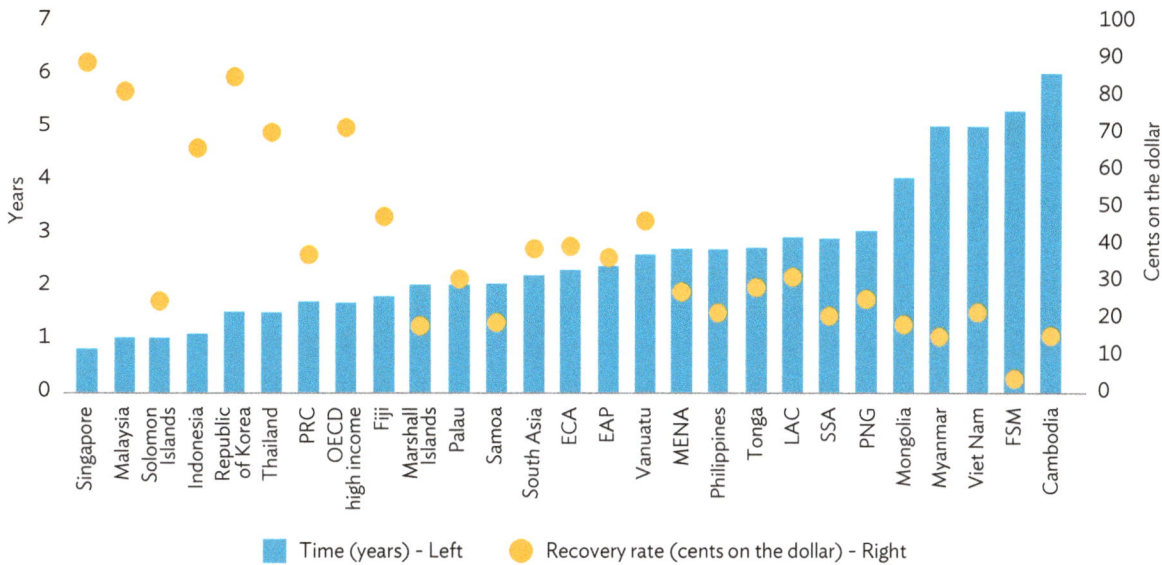

Time (years) - Left   Recovery rate (cents on the dollar) - Right

EAP = East Asia and Pacific, ECA = Europe and Central Asia, FSM = Federated States of Micronesia, LAC = Latin America and Caribbean, MENA = Middle East and Africa, OECD = Organisation for Economic Co-operation and Development, PNG = Papua New Guinea, PRC = People's Republic of China, SSA = Sub-Saharan Africa.

Source: World Bank 2021.

Figure 10: **Ease of Resolving Insolvency**

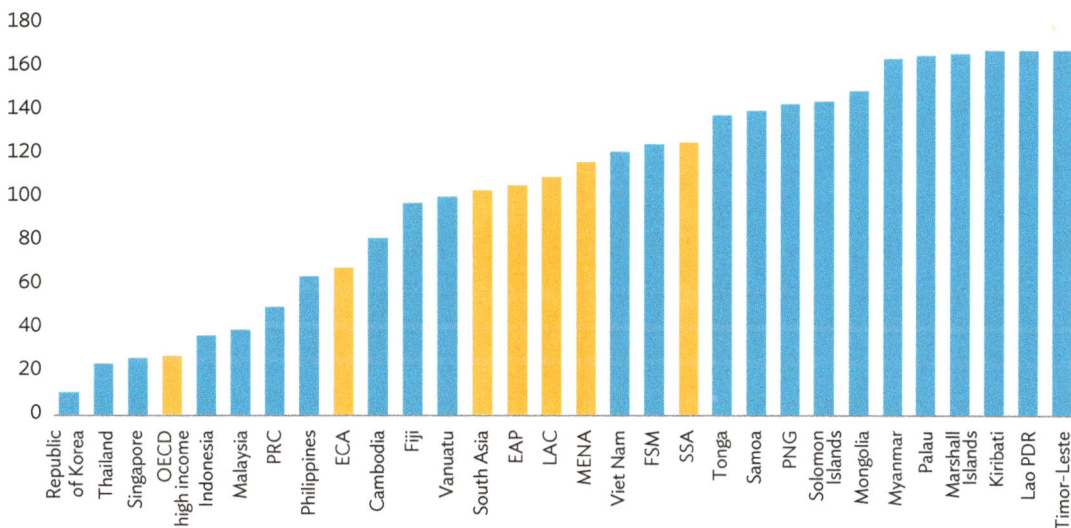

EAP = East Asia and Pacific, ECA = Europe and Central Asia, FSM = Federated States of Micronesia, LAC = Latin America and the Caribbean, Lao PDR = Lao People's Democratic Republic, MENA = Middle East and Africa, OECD = Organisation for Economic Co-operation and Development, PNG = Papua New Guinea, PRC = People's Republic of China, SSA = Sub-Saharan Africa.

Note: Orange bars refer to regional economies.

Source: World Bank 2021.

The *Resolving Insolvency* index relates to the time, cost, and outcome of insolvency proceedings involving domestic legal entities (Figure 10). The Republic of Korea, Thailand, and Singapore rank at the top, and even better than some OECD high-income jurisdictions, while the average rank for the whole East Asia and Pacific is comparable to that in South Asia, Latin America, and the Caribbean.

3.2 Legal Framework on Nonperforming Loan Management and Settlement

The importance of establishing a comprehensive legal and regulatory framework that defines the roles, responsibilities, and rights of various stakeholders, including investors, creditors, and borrowers, cannot be overemphasized. This framework should provide clarity in the definition and classification of NPLs, and it should also address critical aspects such as ownership rights and transferability, enforcement mechanisms, and incentives required to facilitate trading within the market. When specialized laws are enacted to address this issue, it should also try to resolve issues that may arise due to conflicts with existing laws and regulations. Such a framework ensures not only the smooth functioning of NPL trading but also safeguards against potential legal conflicts and uncertainties that could hinder the effectiveness of trading.

3.2.1 Republic of Korea's Legal Systems for Nonperforming Loan Resolution

In essence, NPLs can be characterized as debts arising under a loan contract and as such the Act on Registration of Credit Business and Protection of Finance Users (Loan Business Act) generally applies to NPLs in the **Republic of Korea**. The Loan Business Act regulates the loan industry by outlining registration and supervision requirements for loan and brokerage businesses, and it addresses illegal debt collection and interest rate practices, aiming to foster the industry's healthy development and safeguard financial service users. Since its 2002 inception, the Act has been frequently updated to adapt to the Republic of Korea's changing financial environment, with recent 2021 amendments by the Financial Services Commission emphasizing stronger measures against unlawful lending practices.

The Loan Business Act categorizes "loan business" into two main components: money lending (including activities like loaning money and securing collateral) and debt purchase and collection business (which involves the collection of debts originating from loan agreements acquired from registered lending companies or financial institutions). To engage in the debt purchase and collection business, individuals or entities not classified as financial institutions must register with the Financial Services Commission (where the practice is entrusted to the Financial Supervisory Service). It is important to emphasize that the Loan Business Act's definition of debt purchase and collection business specifically pertains to the collection of debts whose ownership has been transferred from another registered lending company or financial institution, excluding KAMCO from these categories.

Other laws that apply more specifically to NPL-related issues in the Republic of Korea are (i) the Act on the Efficient Disposal of Nonperforming Assets of Financial Companies and the Establishment of Korea Asset Management Corporation (KAMCO Act), which governs the resolution of NPLs by KAMCO; (ii) the Act on Asset-Backed Securitization (ABS Act), which regulates the asset-backed securitization of NPLs by ABS special purpose companies; and (iii) the Korea Housing Finance Corporation Act, which regulates the securitization of residential mortgage debts by the Republic of Korea Housing Finance Corporation.

KAMCO, established as a quasi-governmental entity under the KAMCO Act, is pivotal in restructuring NPLs held by financial institutions and in supporting the recovery of insolvent businesses. Although its origins trace back to 1961, it was not until the enactment of the KAMCO Act in 1997 that the present form of KAMCO emerged, essentially rebranding its predecessor. To assist financial institutions burdened by a rapid increase in NPLs following the Asian financial crisis in 1997, KAMCO played a critical role by purchasing these NPLs with emergency funds, effectively providing a financial lifeline. However, KAMCO needed to dispose of the acquired NPLs to generate funds for further acquisitions, as the emergency funds were quickly depleted with continuous inflow of NPLs. KAMCO used several methods to dispose of the acquired NPLs. These included traditional methods such as competitive auctions, collection of rescheduled repayments, and recourse to the original seller. They also included more innovative methods such as bulk sales and individual sales to domestic and international buyers and issuing asset-backed securities, which launched an important new market in the Republic of Korea.

In 1998, the National Assembly of the Republic of Korea passed the ABS Act, which was instrumental in facilitating NPL restructuring, allowing for asset-backed securitization through special purpose companies, thus simplifying investor access to loan cash flows and overcoming previous legal and procedural hurdles. It provided critical exemptions and procedural simplifications, such as bypassing the Commercial Act's bond issuance limits and the Trust Act's approval requirements, and introduced tax exemptions for certain securitized assets, significantly easing the securitization process.

3.2.2 Evolution of Viet Nam's Nonperforming Loan Resolution Mechanism

No regulation covers securitization in **Viet Nam** and hence only two methods of debt trading are allowed: direct negotiation and auctions. And the market for NPLs is nascent. This is clear from the absence of standardized loan valuation practices and mechanisms for information disclosure, coupled with limited professional brokers, independent asset appraisers, and other financial institutions such as insurance companies, investment funds, pension funds, and securities companies. The legal framework for NPL trading and resolution is therefore still evolving, although significant progress has been made in recent years (Box 1).

Box 1: Evolution of the Legal and Regulatory Framework for Nonperforming Loans in Viet Nam

i.   **Establishment of asset management companies owned by credit institutions (2001):** Viet Nam introduced "debt and asset management companies" owned by commercial banks in 2001 through Decision 150/2001/QD-TTg and Decision 1390/2001/QĐ-NHNN, in which asset management companies focus on managing the nonperforming loans (NPLs) of their parent banks.

ii. **Establishment of Debt and Asset Trading Corporation (2003):** In 2003, Decision No. 109/2003/QD-TTg established the Debt Sale and Purchase Company for State-Owned Enterprises. It transformed into the Debt and Asset Trading Corporation in 2010 (Circular No. 135/2015/TT-BTC increased its capital). Decree No. 129/2020/ND-CP and Circular No. 42/2021/TT-BTC refined the Debt and Asset Trading Corporation's functions and operations.

iii. **Establishment of the Vietnam Asset Management Company (2013):** The Vietnam Asset Management Company (VAMC) was formed under Decree No. 53/2013/ND-CP, addressing NPLs from Vietnamese banks. VAMC helps resolve bad debts, foster credit expansion, and enhance the economy. Its activities include acquiring NPLs with or without collateral, debt recovery, restructuring, asset management, and consultancy. Commercial banks with NPL ratios exceeding 3% of total outstanding debts are required to sell/transfer excessive NPLs to VAMC, with provisions and potential restructuring as approved by the State Bank of Vietnam.

continued on next page

Box 1 *continued*

iv. **Debt trading laws (2016):** Decree No. 69/2016/ND-CP (Decree 69) introduced criteria for debt trading businesses in Viet Nam. The Law on Investment amendment in 2020 removed these conditions, allowing domestic entities to engage in debt trading without restrictions. Foreign ownership in Viet Nam's debt/NPL trading sector may, in practice, require further consultation with licensing authority.

v. **Resolution 42 (2017):** Resolution 42, enacted on 15 August 2017, addressed NPL management limitations by allowing their disposition at market values and broadening the range of entities eligible for NPL transactions. It facilitated the disposal of NPLs below book value, in line with market prices, and expanded the types of organizations that could engage in NPL acquisitions, including those without specific trading licenses. Additionally, it simplified security interest enforcement, enabling direct actions by VAMC or credit institutions under certain conditions, bypassing the need for judicial or executive authority intervention. However, this resolution lapsed on 31 December 2023.

vi. **New Law on Credit Institutions (2024):** The National Assembly of Vietnam passed an amendment to the Law on Credit Institutions (LCI) on 18 January 2024, which becomes effective as of 1 July 2024 (New LCI). The New LCI, inspired by Resolution 42, has a new chapter (Chapter XII) on management of NPLs and secured assets. However, it does not reincorporate Resolution 42's provisions regarding the rights of the lenders and VAMC to seize secured assets.

Source: Compiled by authors.

3.2.3 Nonperforming Loan Definition and Classification

In the **Republic of Korea**, the KAMCO Act defines NPLs as loans, guarantees, and other similar receivables arising from credit transactions by financial companies, including banks, which have not been repaid in the normal course due to insolvency or other reasons and for which recovery measures or loan management is required or which are recognized by the board of directors pursuant to Article 22 of the Act as cases where a substantial risk has arisen or is likely to arise in the recovery of the receivables. This latter is based on the management, financial condition, and expected cash flow of the debtor (Article 2, No. 2 of the Act).

In addition, NPL falls under the definition of "debt under a loan contract" as stipulated in the Loan Business Act as discussed above, and loans below "substandard" are classified as NPLs. Banks classify their loan portfolio into five categories: normal, precautionary, substandard, doubtful, and estimated loss. Loans overdue for more than 3 months are classified as *substandard*, overdue for more than 3 months but less than 12 months as *doubtful*, and overdue for more than 12 months as *estimated loss* (Article 27 and Appendix 3 of the Banking Business Supervision Regulations).

Viet Nam has also adopted similar definitions and classification of NPLs. As per Circular 11/2021/TT-NHNN (Circular 11) issued by the SBV, NPLs refer to debts categorized in groups 3, 4, and 5, the classification of which depends on several criteria, including the repayment ability of the debtor and the overdue period: (i) "group 3 (sub-standard debts)" include debts overdue for 91 days to 180 days, (ii) "group 4 (doubtful debts)" include debts overdue for 181 days to 360 days, and (iii) "group 5 (potentially irrecoverable debts)" include debts overdue for over 360 days. Group 2 (debts subject to attention) include debts overdue for 90 days and group 1 (standard debts) include debts overdue for less than 10 days.

3.2.4 Regulatory Oversight

It is important to designate a regulatory body with the authority to oversee and monitor NPL trading as well as the activities of NPL trading platforms and to set up reporting requirements for platform operators to regularly submit information to regulators. It is equally important to implement mechanisms for compliance with legal and regulatory requirements.

In the **Republic of Korea**, the Financial Services Commission is primarily responsible for setting policies and regulations in the financial market, while the Financial Supervisory Service is the integrated financial supervisory authority responsible for supervision, inspection, and enforcement to ensure that financial institutions operate within the established framework. Both organizations work together to maintain the stability and integrity of the financial system in the Republic of Korea, with the Financial Services Commission providing strategic direction and the Financial Supervisory Service executing regulatory oversight and enforcement activities. Regarding the loan business, including debt purchase and collection business, financial institutions and registered lending companies are subject to inspection by the Financial Supervisory Service and are required to submit regular, semi-annual business reports to the Financial Services Commission (Article 12[4] of the Loan Business Act). For securitization under the ABS Act, it is required to register the ABS plan with the Financial Services Commission (whose authority is entrusted to the Financial Supervisory Service) (Article 3[1] of the ABS Act). Upon transfer of the securitized assets, the transfer must be registered (Article 6[1] of the ABS Act) and disclosed to the public (Article 9[1] of the ABS Act).

In **Viet Nam**, the SBV plays a key role in regulating the financial sector. This includes monetary policy management, foreign exchange management, and banking inspection and supervision pursuant to the Law on the State Bank of Viet Nam, Decree No. 123/2016/ND-CP of 1 September 2016 of the government—stipulating the functions, tasks, mandates, and organizational structures of the ministries and ministerial-level agencies—and to Decree No. 101/2020/ND-CP of 28 August 2020 of the government amending and supplementing a number of Articles of Decree No. 123/2016/ND-CP, and other specific tasks and mandates. In relation to NPL management and settlement, SBV is responsible, among other things, for the promulgation and announcement of regulations, enforcement decrees and circulars related to NPL management and settlement, and taking control measures over credit institutions with significant NPLs, which can include restructuring, mergers, or liquidation to address NPL-related issues. SBV is also responsible for organizing the credit information system and providing credit information services, performing management over the credit information activities, and analyzing credit ratings of legal entities and individuals.

In 2013, the VAMC was launched following Decree No. 53/2013/ND-CP to deal with NPL issues in Viet Nam. VAMC is a 100% state-owned one-member limited liability company established by the SBV with the specific business purpose of purchasing NPLs from credit institutions. VAMC is given broad authority to deal with NPLs in a number of aspects, including (i) acquisition of NPLs from credit institutions, including NPLs with collaterals by issuing special bonds or with its own funds; (ii) debt recovery, collection, settlement, and eventual divestiture of debts and security assets, and facilitation of debt restructuring via rescheduling repayment terms, conversion of debt into equity, and other relevant mechanisms; (iii) oversight and supervision of purchased NPLs and collateral, participation in the management, and restructuring and provision of consultancy; (iv) engaging in the auction process; and (v) nomination of individuals to participate in the management and administration of credit institutions.

3.3 Regulatory Landscape for Nonperforming Loan Trading

Navigating the regulatory landscape for the sale and purchase of NPLs and collateral assets is complex but crucial not only to ensure legal compliance but also to foster confidence among interested parties and maintain the integrity and viability of NPL trading market.

3.3.1 Ownership and Transferability of Nonperforming Loans

In the **Republic of Korea**, the Loan Business Act and its Enforcement Decrees outline a limited set of individuals or entities eligible to acquire debts under loan contracts, including NPLs, from lending companies or financial institutions established and operating in accordance with relevant laws. Specifically, only lending companies that have registered under the Loan Business Act, financial institutions established and operating in compliance with the country's relevant laws, KAMCO, the Korea Housing Finance Corporation, and other entities specified in the Loan Business Act are permitted to purchase NPLs from lending companies and financial institutions authorized or licensed to engage in loan activities under applicable laws. Consequently, lending companies and financial institutions established and operating in accordance with laws are prohibited from transferring NPLs to any individual or entity not explicitly listed as a permitted transferee. Additionally, lending companies are likely restricted from acquiring NPLs from unregistered lending companies for engaging in NPL collection activities.

In **Viet Nam**, credit institutions and foreign bank branches are specifically permitted to sell and transfer their debts (including NPLs), along with attached rights and obligations, to legal entities as well as individuals, including other credit institutions and foreign bank branches that have obtained approval for debt trading from SBV and other organizations and individuals (including residents and nonresidents). VAMC also acquires NPLs from commercial banks in Viet Nam and is authorized to sell and transfer those NPLs to legal entities and individuals, including purchasers who are not specifically engaged in debt trading business.

Circular 09/2015/TT-NHNN of the SBV dated 17 July 2015 as amended by Circular 18/2022/TT-NHNN stipulates that debt purchasers, including nonresidents and nonbank purchasers, will inherit all rights and obligations of the seller. Consequently, debt purchasers will be able to collect debts from borrowers and to take measures to enforce security interests attached to the debt, subject to fulfilment of the procedures necessary for the transfer of security interest under the laws on secured transactions as explored in more detail in section 4 below. In addition, Circular 09 clarifies the debt purchaser's right to request the debt seller to provide information about the purchased debt, including details related to the creation and management of debt and all related documents and demand the debt seller to complete the transfer procedures and comply with its obligations.

3.3.2 License, Permits, and Approvals for Nonperforming Loan Trading

In the **Republic of Korea**, under the Loan Business Act, collecting debts under loan contracts purchased from lending companies and financial institutions (debt purchase and collection business) is considered a loan business, as discussed in section 3.3.1. An entity that is not a bank, financial institution, or other entities explicitly mentioned in the Act, such as KAMCO, must register with the Financial Services Commission to engage in the debt purchase and collection business (Article 2[1], Article 3[3][2] of the Loan Business Act). A person registered as a lending company can purchase loans in accordance with Article 9[4][3] of the Loan Business Act.

In addition, only lending companies with assets exceeding W10 billion ($7.7 million) as of the end of the previous business year with a loan balance of W5 billion ($3.9 million) or more are subject to anti-money laundering obligations under the Specified Financial Information Act (Article 2, Paragraph 14 of the Enforcement Decree of the Specified Financial Information Act). Lending companies that do not meet the foregoing requirements are not subject to anti-money laundering obligations, including know-your-customer (KYC) requirements. When a financial institution subject to anti-money laundering obligations under the Specified Financial Information Act purchases NPLs, it is required to go through KYC process for each individual borrower. However, KYC can be omitted if the financial institution takes appropriate actions such as obtaining KYC records, receiving a guarantee on KYC from the transferor institution, and conducting a sampling check on relevant data (Response to Request for Statutory Interpretation [230119]).

Under the current legal framework in **Viet Nam**, NPL trading is no longer a conditional business. In 2016, the government had introduced Decree No. 69/2016/ND-CP (Decree 69) outlining the prerequisites for engaging in debt trading business in Viet Nam, including minimum capital requirements, internal governance structures, staff qualifications, and established experience. Nevertheless, subsequent to the amendment of the Law on Investment in 2020, which took effect on 1 January 2021, Decree 69 has become obsolete. Accordingly, under the existing legislative framework, debt trading business no longer falls into the classification of conditional business. Consequently, domestic enterprises are now authorized to conduct debt trading operations without being subject to the conditions previously applied under Decree 69.

In light of the current regulations of Viet Nam, particularly Circular 09/2015/TT-NHNN and Circular 18/2022/TT-NHNN of the SBV, it is established that the debt purchasers inherit all rights and obligations of the original creditor, such as the credit institutions and VAMC. This includes the right to recover debts from the borrowers and enforce security interests attached to the debt. Given these regulatory provisions, purchasers of NPLs will be able to perform debt collection activities either independently using their own resources or by engaging certified legal advisors in taking various legal measures such as initiating legal actions against defaulting borrowers, executing foreclosure on collateral, or pursuing other judicial measures to recover the outstanding amounts in compliance with law.

3.3.3 Challenges in Foreign Investor Engagement in Nonperforming Loan Settlement

In the **Republic of Korea**, as discussed in section 3.3.1, registered lending companies and financial institutions are permitted to transfer their NPLs for collection activities only to a certain limited set of purchasers specifically listed in the Loan Business Act.

Foreign financial institutions and foreign entities are not included in the list of buyers who can acquire NPLs from the registered lending company or the financial institution in the Republic of Korea. Accordingly, foreign financial institutions are required to register as a lending company under the Loan Business Act in order to purchase NPLs from another registered lending company or a financial institution in the Republic of Korea by satisfying certain requirements and conditions, including the following: (i) being a corporation, (ii) having capital of at least W500 million ($385,000), (iii) completing education related to lending, (iv) owning a fixed place of business, and (v) not having a major shareholder who has been criminally punished for violating financial laws in the past 5 years. These requirements apply equally to foreigners and corporations with foreign major shareholders.

The restrictions on transfer of NPLs for debt purchase and collection business described above apply to the transfer of NPLs by registered lending companies and financial institutions. The same restrictions do not apply to the transfer of NPLs by KAMCO. There is no similar restriction under the KAMCO Act for the transfer of NPLs from KAMCO to other persons or entities, including foreign entities.

It is also notable that amendments to the Enforcement Decree and Supervisory Regulations of the Loan Business Act are being pursued in which foreign financial companies will be permitted to purchase NPLs in certain cases. These include (i) transferring foreign currency corporate loans provided by syndicate lenders; (ii) transferring foreign currency corporate loans related to trade finance from domestic branches of foreign financial institutions to their headquarters, branches, or affiliates; and (iii) transferring foreign currency corporate loans provided by domestic branches of foreign financial institutions to their headquarters, branches, or affiliates in the event of closure or liquidation of domestic branches of foreign financial institutions.

Viet Nam's legal framework generally and broadly allows for debt trading, but certain ambiguities exist, particularly related to the involvement of foreign investors.

- **Permissibility of debt trading by foreign investors:** Viet Nam currently allows unrestricted trading of debts for domestic enterprises, but there is no commitment to market access for foreign investors in the debt trading sector. However, based on investment laws, foreign investors can have access to the market on par with domestic investors if there are no legal restrictions, which is currently the case. It is worth noting that foreign ownership in Viet Nam's debt/NPL trading sector may require consultation with the licensing authority as a standard practice.

- **Foreign loan issue:** Circular 09/2015 permits nonresident organizations and individuals to purchase debts, but foreign investors acquiring onshore NPLs might be classified as *offshore lenders*, necessitating a foreign loan registration with SBV, lacking clear guidance.

- **Constraints on real estate ownership and holding security interest:** Foreign investors encounter limitations in acquiring real estate or establishing security interests over real estate properties, as only the credit institutions are eligible to establish security interest on land and attached assets under the Law on Land. Further, foreign entities and individuals are generally precluded from directly owning the land use rights and assets attached to land, with limited exceptions for residential houses under the Law on Residential Housing.

- **Registration requirements for movable assets:** Registering movable assets involves complex processes for certain assets, complicating foreign investments. This includes vehicles, vessels, aircraft, and culturally significant items.

- **Impediments to acquiring local companies:** Foreigners buying local firms must navigate various legal considerations, including World Trade Organization commitments, registration for capital contributions/share purchases, and adjustments in company ownership.

- **Restrictions in debt-equity swaps:** Debt-equity swaps, which can be considered an NPL investment method, entail several considerations, including limits on interest accrual, limits on declaration of dividends on equity, and a foreign ownership cap that may be applicable for specific business lines engaged by target companies, etc.

3.4 Enforcement of Security Interest

As the effective enforcement of security interests is essential to facilitate an NPL trading market, this section discusses registration and enforcement of security interests relating to NPLs, including creditor rights and the legal and regulatory environment for effective resolution and settlement of security interests.

3.4.1 Types of Security Interest and Registration

There is no specific regulation regarding the type of collateral for NPLs in the **Republic of Korea**; the general laws such as the Civil Act and the Civil Execution Act apply, as detailed below. However, in the case of asset-backed securitization (ABS) under the ABS Act, the ABS Act provides a special exception regarding the acquisition of a pledge or mortgage. ABS is a financial transaction structure that allows asset holders to raise funds by issuing securities based on NPLs and selling them to investors. The ABS Act recognizes special exceptions related to the transfer of claims, mortgages, etc., to facilitate efficient asset securitization. If the loan being transferred or entrusted pursuant to the ABS plan is secured by a pledge or mortgage, the ABS-special-purpose company acquires the pledge or mortgage upon registering the transfer of assets with the Financial Services Commission (Article 8[1] of the Act).

As for other cases, the transferee must follow legal procedures for that security to acquire such security interest. Typically, for real estate, security rights are established through creation of a mortgage, and registration is required for the establishment and transfer of a mortgage. If the debtor fails to repay the debt, or any other event triggers execution of the security right, the creditor (mortgagee) can apply for a voluntary auction of the mortgaged real estate. The creditor can then be repaid from the proceeds of the sale achieved through the auction.

In **Viet Nam**, the law recognizes various types of secured transactions, including pledges and mortgages over property. Collateral used to secure loans can be categorized into immovable properties (such as land and buildings), movable properties (including cash and assets), and future assets, with the exception of future land use rights.

Certain secured transactions require mandatory registration for legal effectiveness, like mortgages over land use rights (registration over the system of land registry), aircraft, and vessels. Online registration of security transactions is possible through the National Registration of Secured Transaction system (except land use rights, assets attached to land, rights to use sea areas, assets attached to sea areas, and listed/registered securities), and online registration for transportation vehicles (except aircraft and vessels) is planned for 2024.

Transferring security interest to new creditors may require agreement amendments, notarization, or updates to registration records. Security interests become effective against third parties through registration or possession of collateral, with priority determined by the order of these events. In cases of competing security interests, priority follows the sequence of events establishing third-party effectiveness. If all security interests are ineffective, creation order determines priority, but this order can be adjusted by agreement among secured parties.

3.4.2 Enforcement of Security Interest

Enforcement of security interest may involve legal challenges in any jurisdiction, including the Republic of Korea and Viet Nam. Following are some common legal challenges that make it difficult to resolve NPLs:

i. Complex legal procedures

Enforcement often involves complex legal procedures, which may vary from one jurisdiction to another. Understanding and navigating these procedures correctly can be challenging.

In the **Republic of Korea**, there are no special rules for the enforcement of security interests of NPLs. The security is enforced according to procedures applicable for that security interest. For example, for a mortgage, an auction procedure is conducted in accordance with the Civil Execution Act of the Republic of Korea. Specifically, if a creditor (secured party) requests an auction, they must submit an application for voluntary auction along with documents (including a certificate of registered matters) detailing the creditor/debtor/owner, secured right, the subject property of the security interest, etc. After the court decides to initiate the auction, creditors with rights to distribution must file for distribution (those who have completed registration before the auction decision can participate in the distribution process without separate application). The proceeds from the auction are then distributed to the creditors, including registered secured parties.

Under Resolution 42 in **Viet Nam**, creditors had specific rights to seize collateral assets under certain conditions, including clear agreements, compliance with registration, no legal disputes, and notification obligations. This resolution also allowed for simplified court procedures for asset seizure disputes. However, as of 1 January 2024, Resolution 42 was abolished, and the New Law on Credit Institutions (LCI), despite introducing a chapter on NPL and secured asset management, does not explicitly reiterate the right for lenders or VAMC to seize secured assets, leaving a legal gap in this area.

ii. Notification requirements

Many jurisdictions require strict adherence to notification requirements before seizing and disposing of collateral. Failure to comply with these requirements can lead to legal disputes and challenges.

In the **Republic of Korea**, when applying for an auction to enforce a security interest, the secured party must specify the details of the creditor and debtor, the property subject to the security interest, and the debt subject to the auction. The auction commencement decision must be served on the debtor or registered in accordance with the procedures prescribed by the Civil Execution Act. It is notable that in case NPLs are managed by KAMCO, the KAMCO Act stipulates a streamlined process for auction proceedings by stipulating that any notice or service required for auction proceedings under the Civil Execution Act of the Republic of Korea will be deemed to have been made if it is sent to the address recorded in the real estate register (including the address entered in the resident registration card) at the time of the application for auction (Article 45[2][1] of the Act).

Viet Nam law requires notifying the securing party, other secured parties, and collateral holders before seizing and disposing collaterals. Notices must be sent in advance, usually 10 days for movable properties and 15 days for immovable properties, except in cases of imminent collateral damage. Failure to notify may result in compensation.

iii. Bankruptcy proceedings

If the debtor files for bankruptcy, it can complicate the enforcement process. Bankruptcy proceedings may take precedence over the enforcement of security interest, and creditors may need to participate in the bankruptcy proceedings to protect their interests.

In the **Republic of Korea**, creditors can also apply for the commencement of rehabilitation proceedings under the Debtor Rehabilitation Act. If a rehabilitation proceeding is commenced, the creditors must report their claims and security interests to the court and receive reimbursement of their claims and security interests in accordance with the court's rehabilitation plan. The court decides to initiate rehabilitation proceedings upon request from the debtor, creditor, or shareholders, and appoints an administrator to oversee the debtor's business and asset management. Creditors and secured parties must file their claims within a set period, and direct enforcement of these claims is suspended. The administrator devises a rehabilitation plan, reflecting the debtor's assets and the submitted claims, which may adjust the rights of all parties involved.

Under the Law on Bankruptcy of **Viet Nam**, the creditors of unsecured claims and partly secured claims have the right to initiate bankruptcy proceedings, but secured creditors are required to await the outcome of the creditors' meeting (composed of unsecured creditors) in order to proceed with asset settlement. The process can be lengthy, spanning several months from the receipt of the decision to initiate bankruptcy procedures to the convening of the first creditors' meeting. Further, the Law on Bankruptcy mandates asset inventory and valuation. In order to carry out this task, an asset management officer is appointed, but this individual may require additional time to study the documents relating to the debtor company. As a result, this can lead to further delays in both the asset inventory and valuation process and the overall bankruptcy proceedings.

iv. Debtor challenges and defense strategies

Debtors may challenge the enforcement of security interest on various grounds, such as claiming that the collateral's value has been underestimated or that the enforcement process is unfair. Also, debtors may employ various legal strategies to delay or challenge the enforcement of security interests, such as filing counterclaims or seeking injunctive relief.

In the **Republic of Korea**, creditors may seek compulsory auction and take all necessary steps if the debtor does not cooperate with the enforcement of the security right. In the Republic of Korea, if creditors have established a security right, such as a mortgage, they can initiate a voluntary auction process based on that security right. However, if the creditor has not established a security right, they can recover their claims by carrying out compulsory execution through the court, such as seizing the debtor's property. But, to carry out compulsory execution, an enforceable title from the court—such as a final judgment—is required, which can be time consuming. Therefore, if there is a need to urgently preserve the debtor's property before this, provisional measures such as provisional attachment can be taken.

Under the laws of **Viet Nam**, the possessor of secured assets must surrender them as per the seizure notification sent by the creditors. If they do not cooperate, the secured party has the right to initiate legal action and get assistance from local enforcement agencies, but it may take several months to a few years to resolve debtor challenges in legal action.

v. Collateral valuation and disposal

Collateral valuation can be a source of contention and the disposal process can add complexity.

In the **Republic of Korea**, if a debtor fails to fulfill its obligations under a security agreement or security terms and conditions (e.g., upon maturity, acceleration, etc.), the creditor (secured party) may enforce the security interest through an auction and other proceedings.

The auction is conducted by the court overseeing the compulsory auction, and for real estate, the court will have an appraiser assess the value of the property and set the minimum price in consideration of the appraised value (Article 97[1], Article 268 of the Civil Execution Act).

Generally, NPLs acquired by KAMCO are subjected to auction for the recovery of claims through the court auction process. Meanwhile, KAMCO conducts public auction through the OnBid online auction platform (see Chapter 2 for details on OnBid). The subjects of these public auctions include (i) properties seized after failure to pay obligations such as national and local taxes, public charges, fines, etc., for collecting arrears, where the sale of the seized property is entrusted to KAMCO; and (ii) the sale of properties that are collateral for the acquired NPLs and have been acquired by KAMCO through auction.

In **Viet Nam**, the disposal of collateral linked to NPLs involves specific trigger events and methods. These events include the obligator's failure to meet contractual obligations, acceleration due to default, legal requirements, or mutually agreed circumstances. Unless otherwise specified, the secured party can utilize various disposal methods, including auction, direct sale, substitution, or other methods. If the securing and secured parties have no agreement on disposal methods, collateral disposal through auction is used by default, as prescribed by law. Institutions such as the VAMC, Debt and Asset Trading Corporation (Viet Nam) (DATC), commercial banks, and other AMCs, play roles in collateral disposal. VAMC typically manages and disposes of NPL collateral assets by auction, with provisions for negotiations or more auctions if the previous auctions have been unsuccessful. DATC has the authority to handle NPL collateral assets, with support from relevant state agencies for debt recovery. Commercial banks and AMCs can sell NPL collateral assets through multiple methods, including public sales, auctions, sales to VAMC and DATC, or measures such as renovation and business operations. Valuation of NPL collateral assets is crucial and involves a structured process that considers disputes, price regulations, and property types, adhering to legal requirements such as the Law on Property Auction and the Law on Price. Professional appraisal companies, which are required to obtain certifications from the Ministry of Finance, play a significant role in ensuring accurate valuation.

3.5 Reporting and Disclosure Requirements

The **Republic of Korea** does not have specific laws for reporting NPL transactions but mandates disclosure for asset-backed securities under the ABS Act through DART, managed by financial authorities. DART disclosures include transaction structures, asset holders, and securitized asset details, ensuring transparency if NPLs are involved. Additionally, the Republic of Korea maintains various registries for recording security interests across different assets, like real estate, movable property, and intellectual properties, to safeguard transactional clarity and rights protection.

Viet Nam maintains separate databases for registered security interests across asset categories, with the National Registration of Secured Transaction system offering public access to information on movable assets. However, Viet Nam lacks a unified platform for all NPL transactions, except for the VAMC's website, which provides details on collateral and auction notices for NPL assets. Other institutions in Viet Nam publish auction notices for real property collateral related to NPLs but do not offer a comprehensive list of collateral under their management.

3.6 Licensing Requirements for Establishment and Operation of Nonperforming Loan Trading Platforms

In the **Republic of Korea**, the construction and operation of an NPL trading platform that brokers the purchase and sale of NPLs is not required to be licensed or registered under the Loan Business Act or the Financial Consumer Protection Act. Financial regulatory authorities have also taken the position that brokering, arranging, or facilitating a loan purchase and sale contract that does not entail any actual lending is not to be considered as "brokering or facilitating a loan transaction," which otherwise requires registration under the Loan Business Act) (Response to Request for Statutory Interpretation [220054]). However, if the NPL platform arranges the execution of a loan agreement between a lender and a borrower (as opposed to a transaction for the sale of a loan that has already been executed), it may be subject to registration under the Loan Business Act.[12]

Viet Nam has no specific local presence requirement and the need to establish a company within the country for operating an online NPL trading platform depends on the platform's functions and nature. If the platform operates as a "specialized website" offering services in fields such as telecommunications, technology, finance, and banking, there is no specific local presence requirement. This is provided, however, that if the platform incorporates features similar to a social network or news website, the operator must establish a company in Viet Nam and obtain a social network business license, which has specific conditions. Otherwise, there is currently no clear regulation specifically governing the establishment of an NPL trading platform within the context of e-commerce or licenses, permits, and approvals required to establish and/or operate NPL trading platforms in Viet Nam.

Under the Law on Cybersecurity, both domestic and foreign providers of telecommunications, internet, and value-added services operating in Viet Nam's digital realm are subject to data storage and retention obligations, including retention of private and user relationship data for a minimum of 24 months, storage of personal user information, user-generated content, and data on user interactions, and keeping of system logs for network security investigations for at least 12 months.

---

[12]   See section 3.3.2 above for registration requirements for a loan business (including debt purchase and collection business) with the Financial Services Commission under the Loan Business Act.

3.7 Data Privacy and Security Issues

Complying with data privacy laws is critical for platform security and integrity. The stringent laws and regulations protecting sensitive data in NPL transactions can impede rapid NPL trading.

In the **Republic of Korea**, the Personal Information Protection Act, alongside the Credit Information Use and Protection Act, regulates data protection, requiring consent for personal credit information handling and enforcing security measures for its protection. NPL trading platforms need debtor consent to share personal credit information, although amendments like those in the ABS Act, effective 12 January 2024, may waive consent under specific conditions, risking penalties for noncompliance.

Viet Nam's data privacy is governed by laws ensuring consumer data protection, necessitating explicit consent for data collection, and sharing. The Cyber-Information Security Law mandates consent for personal data handling, emphasizing data owners' access rights and the need for prompt breach responses. For NPL trading, creditors must obtain borrower consent for data sharing, with platform operators requiring informed consent for data processing. Cross-border data transfers are scrutinized for national security or privacy risks, underscoring the need to balance data processing with privacy in NPL trading.

3.8 Enforceability of Electronic Contracts

The existence of a legal basis clearly recognizing the formation and enforceability of contracts and agreements entered on the platform, together with a solid foundation for resolving disputes, will greatly contribute to maintaining the integrity of transactions occurring on the electronic NPL trading platforms.

The legal framework regarding electronic contracts in the **Republic of Korea** is governed by the Framework Act on Electronic Documents and Transactions and the Digital Signature Act. In these laws, the concept of an "electronic document" corresponds to that of a "data message" under the United Nations Commission on International Trade Law's Model Law on Electronic Commerce (1996).

In the country, electronic documents and signatures have legal standing similar to written ones if accessible and unaltered since creation or receipt. Financial transaction details must be provided in writing if requested, and certain laws specify delivery methods, like registered mail, that do not allow for electronic documents. Specific electronic signature methods may be required, like in the Electronic Financial Transactions Act, where they must verify actual identity for the transfer of electronic bonds to be legally valid.

Under the legal framework of **Viet Nam**, contracts established through electronic means using "data messages," as defined by the Law on Electronic Transactions, hold the same legal validity as written contracts, as stipulated under Article 119 of the Civil Code of 2015. For an electronic contract to be legally binding in Viet Nam, it must adhere to the conditions outlined in the Law on Electronic Transactions of 2005 (to be replaced by the new Law on Electronic Transactions in effect from 1 July 2024). Key conditions include, but are not limited to the following:

- **Accessibility and usability of data message contents:** The content of the data message shared between the contracting parties should be accessible and usable for future reference as needed.
- **Maintenance of data message format:** The contents of the data message must be stored in the format they were generated, sent, or received in, or in a format that accurately represents the data's content.

- **Identification of origin and details:** The data message must be stored in a manner allowing identification of origin, destination, date, and time of sending and receiving.
- **Compliance with delivery and receipt provisions:** The exchange of data messages between contracting parties must adhere to the regulations stipulated in Articles 15, 16, and 18 of the Law on Electronic Transactions of 2005.

3.9 Tax Incentives

An effective taxation scheme coupled with incentives can enhance NPL trading markets and make platform operations more efficient.

Current laws in the **Republic of Korea** do not offer specific incentives for NPL trading or the operation of NPL trading platforms, except for certain provisions of special treatment that apply to certain companies. For instance, credit rehabilitation services companies, designated by the government for purchasing NPLs and guaranteeing their payment, can record loss reserves as deductible expenses for a limited period. Also, the special purpose companies established under the Asset-Backed Securitization Act can benefit from deductions if they distribute more than 90% of their profits.

Except for these special treatments, general tax rules apply, as outlined below:

- **Corporate income tax:** The corporate tax rate in the Republic of Korea ranges from 9% to 24%, with an additional 10% of corporate income subject to local income tax. As noted, credit rehabilitation services companies can claim special exemptions for deductible expenses, while special purpose companies established under the Asset-Backed Securitization Act can claim deductible income.
- **Personal income tax:** The withholding income tax rate for nonresident interest income is 15.4%, which includes local income tax (the same rate applies to interest income earned by foreign corporations).
- **Capital gains tax:** In principle, the capital gains tax on the transfer of bonds to foreign corporations or nonresidents is 11% (including local income tax) on the gross payment, or 22% (including local income tax) on the realized gain. The withholding tax is the responsibility of the party obligated to withhold and pay the tax.

Viet Nam's laws do not provide specific tax incentives related to NPL trading and/or operation of NPL trading platforms, and the companies established, including foreign invested companies, will be subject to various tax obligations, including value added tax (VAT), corporate income tax, personal income tax for employees, and other applicable taxes and fees, dependent on the specific circumstances.

- **Corporate income tax:** Generally, the corporate income tax rate for enterprises operating in Viet Nam stands at 20%, unless the business qualifies for tax incentives or exemptions. Corporate income tax incentives, exemption, or reduction may apply in specific circumstances stipulated by law depending on the industry and the area of operation of the enterprise established in Viet Nam, but specific tax incentives for debt trading businesses are not currently observed. Provision for NPLs is deductible expense when determining the taxable income of an enterprise in its annual financial statement.
- **Personal income tax:** Nonresident individual foreign investors are subject to a 5% personal income tax on the capital investment profit earned from the company in Viet Nam. This is calculated by applying the nonresident's total taxable income from capital investment to the 5% rate. Similar rules and calculation methods apply to residents.

- **Dividend tax:** Under Article 4.6 of the Law on Corporate Income Tax 2008, as amended, dividends received on capital contribution, joint ventures, or associations with domestic enterprises are exempt from taxation.

- **Tax on remittance of profits:** Foreign investors are allowed to remit profits abroad annually (after fulfilling all tax obligations) and upon completion of their investment in Viet Nam. Notably, remitting profits earned from direct investment activities is prohibited if the enterprises' financial statements show accumulated losses after loss carry-forwards in line with corporate income tax law.

- **Capital transfer tax:** If foreign investors transfer their capital or shares to others, they may be liable for corporate income tax at 20%, where the taxable income for such transfers is calculated by subtracting the purchase price and transfer-related expenses from the transfer price.

- **VAT:** Under current regulations, there is no VAT on selling debt, selling collateral of VAMC's NPLs (no similar regulations for private debt trading companies), and selling collateral for loans extended by credit institutions or by judgment enforcement agencies in line with the laws on settlement of secured assets. If the person who owns the collateral, or has it under their name, sells it to repay the debt— or if the credit institution receives the collateral to replace the performance of debt repayment obligations—when selling the collateral, these secured assets are still subject to VAT.

3.10 Cross-border Considerations

Cross-border NPL transactions necessitate compliance with regulatory frameworks in multiple jurisdictions. As each country will have its own set of regulations governing financial transactions, security enforcement laws, and data protection, among other considerations, differences in regulatory frameworks can expose the parties involved to significant legal risks if not handled correctly. To reduce the risks of cross-border transactions involving NPL trading, various legal and regulatory issues should be considered:

- **Jurisdiction and enforcement:** A significant hurdle in cross-border NPL trading may involve jurisdictional issues. If a loan originates in one country and is purchased by an entity in another, questions around enforceability of contract terms, asset seizures, and legal recourse can get complicated.

- **Tax implications:** Tax considerations will be a significant factor in cross-border NPL trading, as different countries have different tax rules concerning capital gains, withholding tax, and transaction taxes. Understanding the tax obligations in both the seller's and buyer's jurisdictions is crucial for effective pricing and profitability analysis.

- **Currency risk:** Given that cross-border transactions often involve multiple currencies, parties are exposed to currency fluctuation risks. Forward contracts or other hedging options can be used to mitigate these risks.

- **Due diligence:** Due diligence in cross-border NPL trading can be labor-intensive and costly, requiring familiarity with foreign languages, accounting practices, and regulatory frameworks. Box 2 summarizes important diligence steps for NPL purchases in Viet Nam.

Box 2: Legal Due Diligence Considerations for Nonperforming Loan Purchases in Viet Nam

Investors must conduct thorough legal and financial due diligence to understand legal and financial status, and associated risks related to nonperforming loans, their collateral, or associated debtors.

Legal due diligence:

- Reviewing loan documentation, including contracts, agreements, and guarantees.
- Evaluating collateral, including type, value, registration status, and perfection.
- Verifying legal ownership and title of assets and checking for encumbrances.
- Examining ongoing legal proceedings, potential risks, and liabilities.
- Ensuring compliance with laws, regulations, and required permits.
- Assessing the financial distress or insolvency status of the debtor.
- Evaluating environmental compliance and land use rights.
- Analyzing contracts affecting financial situation and business operations.

Financial due diligence:

- Verifying outstanding debt amounts, interest rates, and repayment terms.
- Analyzing cash flow history and projections of the borrower.
- Valuating collateral assets and estimating potential recovery value.
- Reviewing financial statements and assessing financial health.
- Evaluating borrower's profitability, viability, and revenue generation.
- Identifying other financial liabilities and contingent liabilities.
- Understanding industry trends and market conditions.
- Assessing historical repayment behavior and financial distress patterns.

Source: Authors' own elaboration.

4 Data Requirements for Trading and Valuing Nonperforming Loans

Investors require different datasets to value NPLs. This chapter analyzes and summarizes how data impact different valuation methodologies for real estate assets and NPLs, based on international valuation standards. It analyzes loan data templates in use for NPLs globally and in selected countries in Asia and the Pacific. It also considers the adequacy of international data templates for NPL transactions and adjustments required to better capture the country-specific information demands to value NPLs accounting for local resolution practices and court auction procedures. The chapter explores ways an NPL transaction platform can help buyers and sellers with data preparation and validation and the automated valuation of NPLs.

Valuing NPLs can be complex due to the unique nature of these financial assets. Various valuation methods are used to assess the value of NPLs, considering factors such as the underlying collateral, borrower creditworthiness, potential recovery rates, market conditions, and, importantly, the data available to the investor or valuer. For new investors to enter the market for NPLs they need to be comfortable that the data at their disposal does not put them at a competitive disadvantage. Naturally, market participants gather information over time spent in the market and hence the natural information disadvantage of new investors must be overcome through a suitable market infrastructure. Competitive markets tend to provide all the relevant information and thus reduce the barrier to entry for new investors.

4.1 Data Requirements for Purchasing Nonperforming Loans

When purchasing NPLs, investors require a variety of data and information to make informed decisions and assess potential risks and returns of NPL investments as summarized in Table 3:

i. Loan information (loan data tape):[13]

■ **Loan characteristics:** Details about the loans, such as loan type (mortgage, consumer, commercial), original and current loan amount, interest rate, maturity date, and currency.

■ **Borrower information:** About the borrowers, including credit history, financial status, location, and available contact information. The sharing of personal data is protected in most countries and may not be disclosed as part of the initial information package for potential investors.

---

[13] Loan data tapes are essential for the sale of portfolios of loans or assets. For the sale of individual loans or assets, a loan data tape is less commonly used. Instead, the sellers prepare a complete information package that includes all information in unstructured form, i.e., without a structured relational database.

Table 3: Typical Data Fields in the Loan Data Tape

Data Tape	Data	Key Fields			
Borrower Tape	• Detailed information on the borrower, including borrower name, type of borrower, legal status, jurisdiction, and historical drawdowns	• Borrower ID • Borrower name • Current balance • Updated property market value • Previous property market value	• Original property market value • Borrower industrial classification • Borrower economic sector	• Primary property use • Borrower region/ jurisdiction • Months in arrears • Borrower status	• Weighted average maturity • Weighted average seasoning • Weighted average interest rate • LTV
Loan Tape	• Detailed information on the loans, including outstanding balance, interest rate, and interest type	• Loan ID • Borrower ID • Current balance • Currency • Completion date	• Loan term • Maturity date • Seasoning • Amortization type	• Payment frequency • Rate type • Reference rate • Margin	• Gross rate • Undrawn commitment • Whether in receivership
Property Tape (if applicable)	• Detailed information on the collateral, including asset type and market value	• Property ID • Borrower ID • Address • Town • District • Region • Postcode • Title numbers	• Property type • Previous market valuation • Date of last valuation • Valuer • Original value • Original valuation date	• Original valuer • Tenure • Year built • Current gross rent • Estimated market rent • Current balance • Net initial yield	• Net equivalent yield • Net reversionary yield • Number of units • Main tenant • Charge • Prior charge amount
Tenancy Tape (if applicable)	• Detailed information on the property and subunits, including tenant names and rental values	• Property ID • Borrower ID • Tenancy ID • Tenant name	• Current gross rent • Estimated historic market rent • Lease expiry date	• Adopted passing rent	• Number of units • Estimated forward market rent
Sales Tracker	• Detailed information on historic and current asset sale processes				
Guarantor Tape	• If loans have guarantees attached, details such as guarantor name, amount, and type are disclosed				
Payment History	• Borrower interest and capital payment history	• Borrower ID • Historical capital payments (since origination) • Historical interest payments (since origination)			

ID = identifier, LTV = loan-to-value.
Source: Deloitte as cited in ADB 2022.

■ **Collateral details:** Information about underlying collateral, such as collateral type, location of immovables, model and serial number of movables, condition, appraised value, and type of appraised value. The legal status of the collateral if subject to enforcement proceedings.

■ **Loan status:** The current financial and legal status of the loans, including payment history, delinquency status, default status and date of default, and any ongoing legal proceedings.

■ **Tenants and guarantors:** Information about tenants of commercial property collateral or guarantors who fully or partially guaranteed payments on the loan.

ii. **Historical performance data (as part of the loan data tape or provided separately):**

■ **Loan performance history:** Historical payment records, delinquency patterns, and any previous attempts at resolution or recovery.

■ **Recovery rates:** Data on recovery rates, liquidation haircuts, cure rates and failure rates from similar NPLs in the past, including both successful and unsuccessful recovery attempts.[14]

---

[14] Cure rates reflect the chance that the borrower recovers and resumes payments on the loan. Failure rates are relevant for NPL where the borrower has agreed on a payment plan but may redefault on the planned payments.

iii. Legal documents and communication (as part of the visual data room used for due diligence):

- **Loan documentation:** Copies of loan agreements, collateral documents, and relevant legal documents related to the loans.

- **Legal status:** Information on ongoing legal proceedings, foreclosure processes, and potential legal barriers to recovery.

- **Collateral status and valuation:** Information on the collateral in the form of appraisal reports (including both open market value and forced sale value/liquidation values), floor plans, maps, and pictures, environmental risks, or energy efficiency.

- **Communication:** A record of all recent communication with the borrower or the courts.

- **Recovery options:** Information on potential recovery strategies that have been tried, such as negotiation of payment plans, discounted payoffs, restructuring, or enforcement procedures.

- **Due diligence reports:** Comprehensive reports of the legal and financial due diligence.

iv. Market data (provided by specialist financial data providers or transaction platforms):

- **Trading prices:** Information about NPL prices, credit spreads and yields, actual sale prices, market prices from other credit markets (e.g., bond, CDS, syndicated loan secondary market, or new loan origination market).

- **Real estate market trends:** Data on property market conditions, local real estate trends, property values, and supply and demand dynamics in the collateral's location.

- **Economic indicators:** Information about the macroeconomic environment, interest rates, unemployment rates, and other factors that may impact borrower repayment capacity.

- **Market research:** Insights into market trends, investor sentiment, and competitive landscape in the NPL investment sector.

v. Credit risk information (provided by third party rating agencies or credit bureaus):

- **Credit reports:** Credit reports of the borrowers, including their credit scores, payment history, outstanding debts, and other credit-related information.

- **Credit scoring models:** Data on credit scoring models used to assess the creditworthiness of borrowers.

- **Collection scores:** Scores describing the chance that a borrower will resume regular payments or express the expected recovery rate.[15]

Collecting and analyzing these types of data enables investors to assess the risk–return profile of NPL investments, develop effective recovery strategies, and make well-informed decisions about acquiring and managing NPL portfolios. Due diligence is critical to understanding the potential challenges and opportunities associated with NPL investments and to structuring deals that align with investors' goals and risk tolerance.

---

[15] Collection scores that express the risk of payment on defaulted claims are less common than credit scores expressing the risk of non-payment. Examples include the Collection Score from Schufa in Germany or recovery ratings from the main credit rating agencies.

4.2 Valuation Methods for Nonperforming Loans

Based on the available data, the nature of the underlying assets, and investor preferences, there are different valuation methods for NPLs:

i. Market approach:

- **Comparable sales method:** This method involves comparing the NPLs to similar loans that have been recently sold or settled. Comparable transactions can provide insights into potential recovery rates based on historical trade data. As NPL price data tend to be scarce, the market approach is rarely applied to NPLs except for claims to high profile borrowers ("fallen angels") that actively trade or for which dealers provide regular market quotations.

ii. Income approach:

- **Discounted cash flow analysis:** The analysis estimates the present value of future cash flows, considering factors like interest rates, discount rates based on return expectation and costs of capital, market trends, the borrower's credit risk, and projected cash flows from the collateral (either from liquidation of the collateral or the income that the collateral generates).

- **Collateral-based approaches:** An independent appraiser determines the current market value of the underlying collateral. This value serves as a basis for assessing the NPL's value. Often the collateral cannot be sold in the open market but is subject to a judicial auction process. In this case, the liquidation value, also known as foreclosure value or forced sale value needs to be estimated which typically involves a valuation haircut to open market values.

iii. Historical recovery rates:

- **Analysis of past recoveries:** Historical data on similar NPLs that have been resolved or recovered in the past can provide insights into potential recovery rates. This approach requires a sufficient volume of comparable cases and is typically used to value consumer claims and unsecured claims to corporates using suitable recovery curves. A recovery curve is the projection of recovery cash flows over time.

- **Credit risk analysis:** Using credit risk metrics like probability of default and loss given default assesses the likelihood of the borrower defaulting on the loan and the potential loss in case of default. These metrics are commonly used by banks to estimate the expected loss on NPLs and for the calculation of loan loss provisions. Bank valuation under international accounting standards (IFRS 9) are a type of hold valuation that differ from the price that an investor would be willing to pay for an NPL.[16]

iv. Scenario analysis and expert judgment:

- **Stress testing:** By subjecting the NPL portfolio to various stress scenarios (e.g., economic downturn, interest rate changes), analysts can estimate the potential impact on recovery rates and value.

- **Advisory inputs:** Engaging financial experts, appraisers, or valuation professionals can provide valuable insights and expert judgment in assessing NPL values.

---

[16] NPL Markets. How to Value Bank Loans in a Crisis. https://nplmarkets.com/how-to-value-bank-loans-in-a-crisis/.

It is important to note that the choice of valuation method often depends on the availability of data, the complexity of the NPLs, and the specific circumstances surrounding the loans and collateral. A combination of multiple methods and thorough analysis is often used to arrive at a valuation for NPLs. Additionally, regulatory and accounting standards may influence the choice of method and the assumptions made during the valuation process.

4.3 Data Templates and Background on Nonperforming Loan Valuation

NPL market participants in Asia and the Pacific currently do not use a single data template for NPL transactions nor for the valuation of distressed assets. In many jurisdictions, including the Republic of Korea and Viet Nam, banks and AMCs use external valuation advisors routinely before transacting at market values.

As an example, in Viet Nam Decree 61/2017/ND-CP provides guidelines for the valuation and sale of NPLs. The starting price for the sale of NPLs is an important aspect of this process and is typically determined through an appraisal process. The decree provides a framework for the valuation and sale of NPLs with the goal of ensuring that the sale process is transparent, fair, and in the best interests of all parties involved.

The decree also sets forth requirements for the sale of NPLs to third-party investors. The sale must be conducted through an open auction or other transparent process, and the starting price must be publicly disclosed in advance. The starting price cannot be lower than the appraised value of the collateral or the book value of the loans, whichever is higher (Hoang Quan Appraisal 2022). The selected appraisal firm must be on the public list of enterprises eligible for price appraisal activities of the Ministry of Finance.

The implementation of bad debts appraisal under the decree faces many difficulties, especially in determining the reserve price of high-value debts and the valuation of high volatility properties such as unbuilt land with doubtful planning permission of incomplete construction projects. The next section explains the valuation of distressed loans backed by real estate.

4.3.1 Background on Valuing Loans Backed by Real Estate

There are multiple valuation methods for loans backed by real estate, which mostly use the appraised value of the real estate collateral as an input. The valuation of performing real estate loans requires the estimation of a suitable discount rate linked to the riskiness of the loan. The riskiness of the loan is often expressed by a rating or probability of default and depends, among other factors, on the value of the collateral. Once defaulted, the loan can be resolved in one of several workout scenarios such as (i) cure/re-performing/restructuring, where the borrower recovers and resumes regular payments possible according to a restructured payment plan; (ii) voluntary sale of the collateral by the borrower; or (iii) a forced sale of the property during a court-driven foreclosure process.[17] The timing and costs related to the different resolution strategies must be estimated to create a discounted cash flow analysis for the loan.

---

[17]   NPL Markets. A Single Integrated Platform to Manage Credit Portfolios and Transactions. https://Nplmarkets.Com/En/News/Article/Lessons-Learnt-From-First-Eba-Npl-Data-Templates.

The valuation of nonperforming real estate loans is based on similar workout scenarios but uses more information that have become available after default of the loan such as whether a legal process has been initiated, whether the borrower is cooperative or whether the borrower and the collateral are part of a bankruptcy procedure. The value of the real estate is a key value driver of the loan and hence an accurate loan valuation requires an accurate and recent valuation of the real estate.

For valuing real estate, different valuation methods apply:

(i)   **Market value:** This method estimates the current market value of the real estate collateral that secures the loan. It is based on recent sales of similar properties in the same area, considering the size, location, condition, and other factors that affect the value of the property. The appraiser may also consider the replacement cost of the property and the income it generates if it is an investment property. The appraiser will consider legal aspects like planning permissions or environmental and technical aspects like energy efficiency.

(ii) **Income approach:** This method is used for loans backed by income-generating properties, such as rental properties. It estimates the value of the property based on the income it generates, taking into account the expected future cash flows, the occupancy rate, the rental rates, and other factors that affect the property's income potential.

(iii) **Cost approach:** This method estimates the value of the real estate collateral by calculating the cost of rebuilding the property from scratch, minus any depreciation. It is often used for new properties or properties that have recently been renovated or upgraded.

(iv) **Broker price opinion:** This method is less formal than a full appraisal and is often used for smaller loans or when time is limited. A broker price opinion is an estimate of the property's value provided by a real estate broker or agent, based on their knowledge of the local real estate market and recent sales of similar properties.

The risk of default or probability of default of a loan backed by real estate can be influenced by several factors:

(i)   **Market conditions:** The performance of the broader real estate market can impact the risk of default on a loan. For example, if there is an oversupply of properties in a specific area or if vacancy rates are high, it may lead to lower rental rates and decreased cash flows, which can increase the risk of default.

(ii) **Property-specific factors:** The risk of default can also be influenced by property-specific factors, such as the property type, location, condition, and occupancy rate. Properties in high-demand locations and those with stable occupancy rates may be less likely to default, while properties in declining areas or those with high vacancy rates may be at higher risk of default.

(iii) **Borrower creditworthiness:** This can also impact the risk of default. Borrowers with strong credit histories and financials are generally considered lower risk, while those with poor credit histories or limited financial resources may be at higher risk of default.

(iv) **Loan-to-value ratio:** This measures the ratio of the loan amount to the value of the property. A higher loan-to-value ratio indicates a greater risk of default, as the borrower has less equity in the property and may be more likely to default if property values decline.

(v)   **Debt service coverage ratio:** The debt service coverage ratio measures the property's ability to generate enough cash flow to cover the loan payments. A lower ratio indicates a greater risk of default, as the property may not be generating enough income to cover the loan payments.

(vi) **Interest rate risk:** The risk of default can also be influenced by interest rate risk. Higher interest rates can raise loan payments and make it more difficult for borrowers to make payments, increasing the risk of default.

The cure rate of a defaulted loan backed by real estate can be influenced by a variety of factors which are similar to the factors that determine the probability of default. To assess these factors that influence the riskiness and valuation of a secured loan, the valuation requires analysis of a variety of data fields. The specific fields may vary depending on valuation method, but common key data fields are included in the following (for a more comprehensive NPL transaction data template, see EBA 2022):[18]

(i) **Property type:** The type of property backing the loan, such as land, office, retail, industrial, or multifamily.

(ii) **Property location:** Including city, state, and neighborhood. Some data tapes provide coordinates to allow use of online maps to show location and surroundings.

(iii) **Property characteristics:** Specific characteristics of the property, such as size, age, and condition.

(iv) **Occupancy rate:** The percentage of the property currently occupied by tenants.

(v) **Rental rates:** Rent being charged to tenants for the property.

(vi) **Operating expenses:** The costs associated with operating and maintaining the property, such as property taxes, insurance, maintenance, and utilities.

(vii) **Cap rate:** The capitalization rate used to estimate the property's value based on its net operating income.

(viii) **Loan terms:** The terms including interest rate, maturity date, and outstanding balance.

(ix) **Borrower creditworthiness:** Including their credit score and financial history.

(x) **Market conditions:** Broader real estate market conditions, including supply and demand, vacancy rates, and rental rates.

4.3.2 The Data Template of the Vietnam Asset Management Company and Korea Asset Management Corporation Platforms

The VAMC-Loan Transaction Platform Branch provides an Excel-based data template for download on their website. The template contains 82 data fields about the selling institution, the borrower, claim and real estate and non-real estate collateral, e.g., transportation equipment. As expected, many VAMC data fields also appear in other international NPL transaction templates (as discussed below), but differences exist. First, the VAMC template does not impose a relational data schema that captures complex multiple-to-multiple relationships between claims, contracts, borrowers, mortgages, collaterals, guarantees, and historical cash flows. If those complex relationships exist, then a two-dimensional Excel sheet may not be suitable to represent multidimensional data. Similarly, KAMCO uses standardized data for NPL purchases that do not follow a complex relational structure and provides relatively little information on the borrowers and the collateral as described further below. Neither the VAMC nor the KAMCO template contain historical cash flow data.

---

[18] NPL Markets. 2023a. Final Draft Implementing Technical Standards from EBA for NPL Transaction Data Templates. https://nplmarkets.com/final-draft-implementing-technical-standards-from-eba-for-npl-transaction-data-templates/.

If the VAMC template was to be used also for the direct sale of commercial real estate assets, then more details about the properties, the tenancy agreements, and tenants would be required. The data template includes descriptive fields on land lease rights that are important in several Asian countries where the land is owned by the state and subject to long-term leases. Some banks in Viet Nam interviewed as part of this study find the VAMC data template too extensive. Both banks and investors agree that some critical fields are missing especially regarding the real estate collateral such as the detailed address and condition of the property, the nature and stage of the legal process (if any), and the type, amount, and source of recent valuations. Importantly, the loan data shared with investors should contain the complete payment history after default or after being classified as nonperforming. Location services are available that translate the exact address to coordinates which can then be accurately displayed on an interactive map.

Real estate assets are commonly listed on the Republic of Korea's OnBid platform and the online information about such real estate is very comprehensive, including pictures, floor plans, land registry documents, location maps, and contact information for the seller to arrange for onsite visits of the real estate prior to the auction.

4.3.3 The Mandatory Data Template in the European Union (EBA Templates)

On 19 October 2023, the new NPL transaction templates from the European Banking Authority (EBA) became mandatory for European banks for NPL portfolio sales after the publication of the implementing technical standards in the official journal of the European Union.

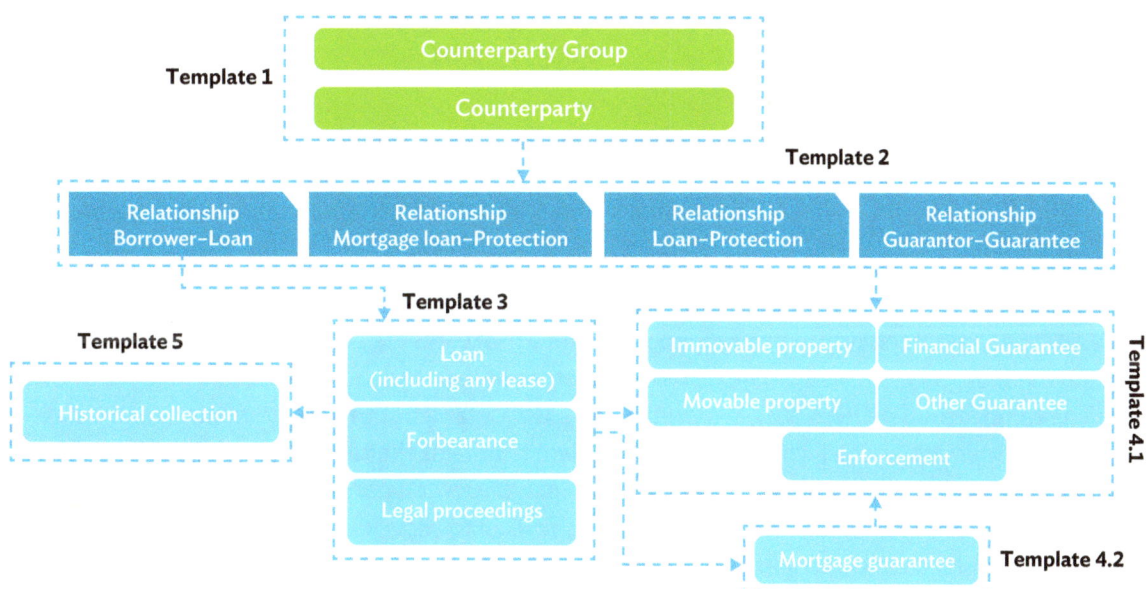

Figure 11: Data Templates for Nonperforming Loan Transactions for European Union Banks

Source: European Banking Authority. https://www.eba.europa.eu/regulation-and-policy/credit-risk/implementing-technical-standards-npl-transaction-data-templates.

The overall template encompasses five sub-templates or tables (Figure 11).[19]

- T1 Counterparty includes data fields describing, borrowers, co-borrowers, borrower groups, and guarantors.

- T2 Relationships covers the relational structure between loans, counterparties, mortgages, properties, other non-property collateral and guarantees.

- T3 Loan includes the fields describing the contracts and claims, including forbearance measures and legal proceedings.

- T4 Collateral and Enforcement includes the information on property and non-property collateral and any enforcement measures.

- T5 Historical Collections includes historical cash flow information.

European NPL transaction platform nplmarkets.com recently reported its experience with transforming the data shared with investors as part of actual NPL portfolio sale on the NPL Markets transaction platform (NPL Markets 2023b). NPL Markets found the following to be important considerations for sellers when working with new regulatory data templates:

(i)   The EBA NPL templates are establishing a common standard for all types of NPL portfolio sales across many jurisdictions. As such, they will differ substantially from nonstandardized data used in prior transactions. Most selling banks will need to provide data fields that they did not provide before and some of their previously provided information is not part of the EBA NPL templates.

(ii)   Sellers should expect a few mandatory data fields that are not readily available. EBA has clarified that the NPL templates are not a regulatory reporting requirement, and the nondelivery of certain mandatory fields will likely not result in sanctions or penalty fees. It remains to be seen, however, how competently authorities in each jurisdiction will monitor the new templates and react to potential noncompliance.

(iii) Creating investor data tapes in the EBA NPL template format is not particularly complex, time-consuming, or expensive compared with the creation of the investor data tapes currently used by sophisticated sellers. Data mapping software can help create the standard data template and run detailed validation checks, which means that creating standard validated template outputs, after the initial setup, can be largely automated.

4.3.4 The Mandatory Data Template in Kazakhstan

Kazakhstan is the only country in Asia and the Pacific introducing a single standard data template as part of accreditation for NPL trading platforms. The use of the online platforms and of the standard data templates will become mandatory when required legislative processes are completed. The design of the Kazakhstan data template is based on the EBA templates for NPL transactions described in the previous section. The template differs from the EBA template in a few details, but key design features and details are maintained. Specifically, the Kazakhstan data template maintains the same five sub-templates T1 through T5 and the classification of each data field into mandatory and nonmandatory. In one change to Kazakhstan's template, the type of borrower data field is revised to allow identification of state-owned enterprises, which play an important role in many Asian countries.

---

[19]   EBA. Implementing Technical Standards on NPL Transaction Data Templates. https://www.eba.europa.eu/regulation-and-policy/credit-risk/implementing-technical-standards-npl-transaction-data-templates.

4.4 A Data Template for Asia and the Pacific Proposed by ADB

The data template proposed by ADB as part of this feasibility study draws on international experience and focuses on portfolio sales to institutional investors. B2C auction platforms selling single assets or single NPLs are not expected to use these templates. The proposed data template for Asia and the Pacific is based on the EBA NPL data templates, with adjustments (Table 4). The three sub-tables of Table 4 show data fields added to the Asian data template and are not present in the EBA NPL templates, split by template T1 Counterparty; T3 Loan; and T4 Collateral, Guarantees, and Enforcement templates, respectively.

Whereas the EBA template refers to different European laws and regulations, these references have been replaced with global international standards in the Asian template. For instance, the Asian template proposes to use international International Standard Industrial Classification of All Economic Activities industry codes (first example in Table 4a). Certain data fields have been added based on user feedback from Asian investors, such as the noted ability to identify state-owned enterprises as borrowers or counterparty groups (Table 4a) or the interest rate margin applicable when the loan is in arrears or in default (Table 4b). As mentioned, because many countries in Asia and the Pacific do not allow freehold ownership of land, the expiry date of land lease rights is an important data field in Asia and the Pacific not present in the EBA template (Table 4c). Overall, however, there are relatively few changes and the proposed template for Asia largely follows the EBA standard.

The Asian NPL transaction data template is available free from the ADB website.[20]

Table 4a: Data Field Additions to the Template T1 Counterparty

Template	Data Field	Description	Field Type
Counterparty	Economic activity of counterparty group	Classification of the counterparty group according to their economic activities	Choice populated by using the classification ISIC Rev 4 codes at level two, three, or four
Counterparty	Type of counterparty	Type of counterparty ("private individual," "individual entrepreneurship," "small and medium business," "corporate business," or "state-owned enterprise")	Choice: (i) Private individual (ii) Individual entrepreneurship (iii) Small and medium business (iv) Corporate business (v) State-owned enterprise
Counterparty	Nationality of counterparty	The main nationality of the private individual counterparty	Choice populated using ISO 20022
Counterparty	Annual EBITDA	Amount of annual EBITDA generated by the corporate counterparty as per the latest available financial statements for year-end or quarterly (audited, and if not then unaudited)	Number

continued on next page

20   International Public AMC Forum. https://ipafasia.org/news-and-data/npl-data/.

Table 4a *continued*

Template	Data Field	Description	Field Type
Counterparty	Date of initiation of legal proceedings	The date on which the legal proceedings, as reported under the field "status of legal proceedings," were initiated. This date must be the most recent relevant date prior to the cut-off date and must only be reported if the field "Status of legal proceedings" has a value other than "No legal actions taken."	dd/mm/yyyy
Counterparty	Stage reached in legal proceedings	Indication of how advanced the relevant legal proceedings have become as a result of various legal steps in the legal proceedings having been completed	Alphanumeric
Counterparty	Proof of claim filed by the seller	Indicator as to whether the institution has filed a claim	Boolean (Yes or No)
Counterparty	Notice for procedure termination	Indicator as to whether the notice of the end of the procedure has been given to the institution and no further collections are expected	Boolean (Yes or No)
Counterparty	Date of obtaining order for possession	Date that the order for possession is granted by the court (in case of mortgage)	dd/mm/yyyy
Counterparty	Legal fees accrued	Total amount of legal fees accrued at the cut-off date	Number
Counterparty	Priority wage claim amount	Total amount of prior ranking claims from employees for wages or pensions	Number
Counterparty	Priority tax or other claim amount	Total amount of prior ranking tax claims	Number

EBITDA = earnings before interest, tax, depreciation, and amortization; ISIC = International Standard Industrial Classification of All Economic Activities; ISO = International Organization for Standardization.
Source: Authors.

Table 4b: Data Field Additions to the Template T3 Loan

Template	Data Field	Description	Field Type
Loan	Contract identifier	Institution's internal identifier to uniquely identify each loan agreement. Each loan agreement must have one contract identifier. This value will not change over time and cannot be used as the contract identifier for any other loan agreement.	Alphanumeric
Loan	Instrument identifier	Institution's internal identifier to uniquely identify each loan under a single loan agreement. Each loan must have one instrument identifier. This value will not change over time and cannot be used as the intrument identifier for any other loan under the same loan agreement. Instrument identifier may be the same as contract number.	Alphanumeric

continued on next page

Table 4b *continued*

Template	Data Field	Description	Field Type
Loan	Amortization type	Type of amortization including principal and interest, as per the latest loan agreement.	Choices: (i) Fixed annuity payments (ii) Fixed principal payments (iii) Fixed bespoke principal schedule (iv) Bullet (v) Other
Loan	Nonperforming category	Nonperforming category to which the loan belongs. Use the choices provided or the categories defined in the applicable jurisdiction.	Choices: (i) Unlikely to pay that are not past-due or past-due <=90 days; N (ii) Past-due >90 days and <=1 year; (iii) Past-due >1 year
Loan	Total past-due amount	Carrying amount of loan that is past due. This amount is always to be reported. "0" is to be reported if the loan was not past due at the cut-off date.	Number
Loan	Legal balance at charge-off date	Total claim amount (including total balance and any accrued interest balance off book) when the loan went into charge-off. A charge-off is the declaration by the institution commonly on unsecured retail when the borrower is severely delinquent, and the institution starts the recovery process officially. In case of closed position, the amount will be zero. The data field is required only when the loan goes into charge-off.	Number
Loan	Charge-off date	Date when the loan first went into charge-off. A charge-off is the declaration by the institution commonly on unsecured retail when the borrower is severely delinquent, and the institution starts the recovery process officially. A charge-off does not mean a write-off the debt entirely.	dd/mm/yyyy
Loan	Loan commitment	Total available credit extended for the loan as at the cut-off date. This includes the undrawn committed part of the loan commitment.	
Loan	Past-due penalty interest margin	Additional margin charged on the past-due portion of the loan according to the loan agreement and applicable as of the cut-off date.	Percentage
Loan	Default penalty interest margin	Additional margin charged on the loan in default according to the loan agreement and applicable as of the cut-off date	Percentage

Source: Authors.

Table 4c: Data Field Additions to the Template T4 Collateral, Guarantee, and Enforcement

Template	Data Field	Description	Field Type
Collateral guarantee and enforcement	Immovable property longitude and latitude of its location	The longitude and latitude separated by comma of the immovable real estate collateral	Alphanumeric, Alphanumeric
Collateral guarantee and enforcement	Tenure	Conditions that the property is held or occupied, e.g., freehold and leasehold (land lease rights)	(i) Freehold, (ii) Leasehold, (iii) Other
Collateral guarantee and enforcement	Remaining term of leasehold or land use right	Remaining in terms in years of the leasehold when "Leasehold" is selected in field "Tenure"	Number
Collateral guarantee and enforcement	Date of issue of certificates of land use right	The Date of Issue of Certificates of Land Use Right	dd/mm/yyyy
Collateral guarantee and enforcement	Immovable property status	The current status of the property. A textual description of the legal and economic status of the property. Example states include Foreclosure, Real Estate Owned, Partial Release, Released, in Special Servicing or another bespoke description.	Alphanumeric
Collateral guarantee and enforcement	Sector of immovable property	Sector which the immovable property is used for. Applicable to all immovable (real estate) collateral	Choices: (i) commercial real estate (CRE) N, (ii) residential real estate (RRE)
Collateral guarantee and enforcement	Percentage complete	The percentage of completion of the construction of the immovable property. Applicable to immovable property under development (i.e., if "No" is reported in the field "Completion of Immovable property").	Percentage
Collateral guarantee and enforcement	Court name	The name of the court where the enforcement proceedings are being held	Alphanumeric
Collateral guarantee and enforcement	Legal status	A detailed description of the legal status of the property collateral	Alphanumeric

Source: Authors.

4.5 Data Quality and Validation

Standardized data templates ease the design and implementation of detailed automated data quality checks. Such checks are crucial for ensuring the reliability and accuracy of the data populated into the template and available NPL trading platform. High-quality data fosters trust among users and keeps due diligence costs manageable. Several levels of verification and validation are recommended to guarantee accurate data suitable for the intended purpose.

i. Field-specific checks:

Automated validation is conducted across all fields in the template to verify data correctness and accuracy. This includes the following:

- Ensuring all required (mandatory) fields in the template are present.
- Identifying and handling duplications of unique fields.
- Counting the number of missing (blank) values within a given field.
- Verifying the format of values, detecting values in incorrect formats.
- Checking that values fall within valid ranges, preventing outliers.

ii. Consistency checks across fields:

Checks are applied to mutually dependent fields within the template to maintain consistency.
For instance:

- The total legal balance must be the sum of principal, accrued interest, and other outstanding amounts (fees, etc.).
- Properties linked to a mortgage in the mortgage table must be present in the table for property collateral.
- If a loan is more than 90 or 180 days past due, it must be flagged as nonperforming, based on regulatory definitions.
- Ensuring collateral-related fields are correctly reported based on collateral type.
- Verifying the alignment of loan-to-value with collateral value and loan balance.

iii. Consistency checks across time:

Checks are conducted to ensure datasets are consistent across multiple time snapshots. These checks are particularly important for the collection of historical data observed at different cutoff dates (snapshots).

iv. Distribution checks:

Distribution checks involve verifying data distributions to identify potential anomalies. Sometimes missing data is masked by the presence of dummy data entries. For instance, if the date of default is set to 2022-01-01 for a large percentage of all loans, then the date of default for those loans is very likely not available, and the reported value is a dummy value.

In summary, quality checks are essential for maintaining accurate and trustworthy data on the NPL trading platform.

4.6 Unstructured Information and Smart Virtual Data Rooms

Detailed information on assets for sale is made available in data rooms, which nowadays are almost always virtual and may be an integral part of an NPL transaction platform. Portfolio sales of NPLs typically require the institutional investors interested in the assets to sign a nondisclosure agreement with the seller and receive access to a data room to review underlying loan documentation, judicial decisions, and other asset related information at a granular level. Sellers use both external (provided by a third party) and internal data rooms. Figure 12 shows some of the steps required to prepare a VDR for due diligence.

Figure 12: Data Room Preparation Activities for Investor Due Diligence

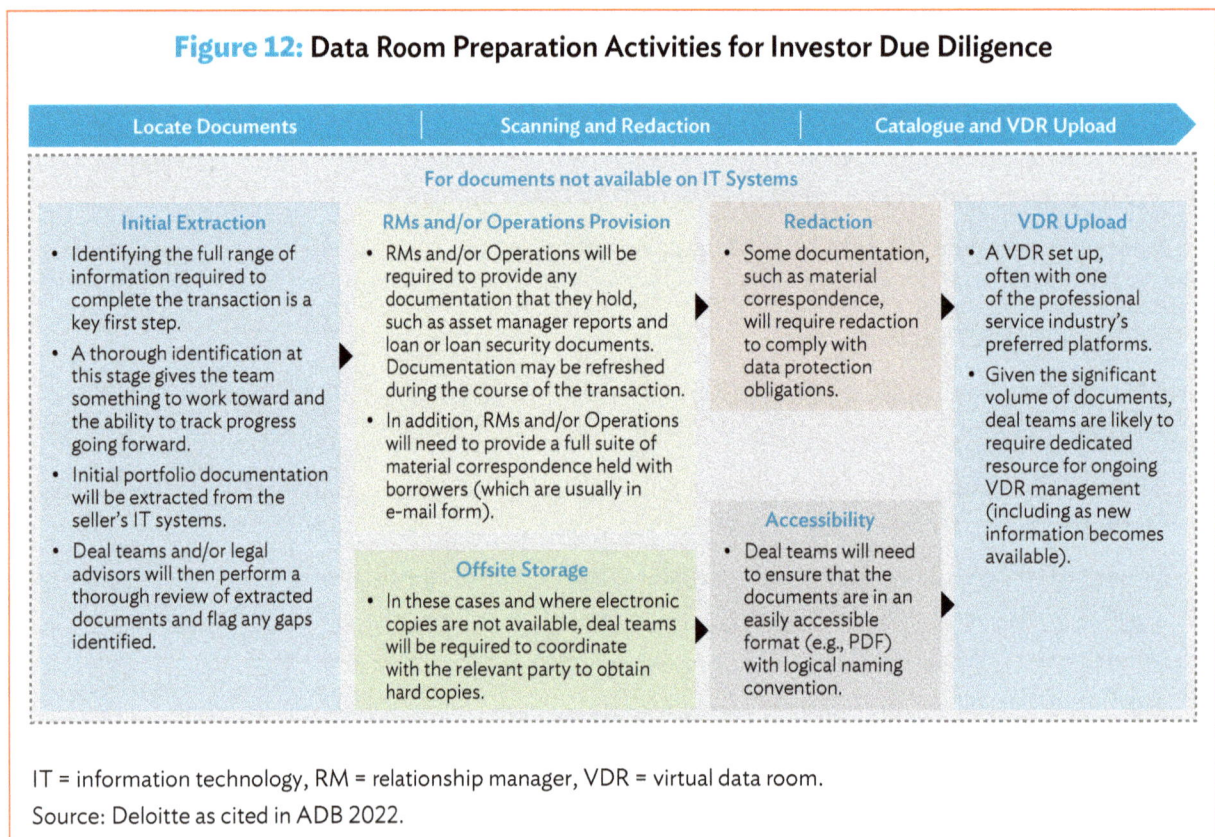

Locate Documents	Scanning and Redaction	Catalogue and VDR Upload

For documents not available on IT Systems

Initial Extraction
- Identifying the full range of information required to complete the transaction is a key first step.
- A thorough identification at this stage gives the team something to work toward and the ability to track progress going forward.
- Initial portfolio documentation will be extracted from the seller's IT systems.
- Deal teams and/or legal advisors will then perform a thorough review of extracted documents and flag any gaps identified.

RMs and/or Operations Provision
- RMs and/or Operations will be required to provide any documentation that they hold, such as asset manager reports and loan or loan security documents. Documentation may be refreshed during the course of the transaction.
- In addition, RMs and/or Operations will need to provide a full suite of material correspondence held with borrowers (which are usually in e-mail form).

Offsite Storage
- In these cases and where electronic copies are not available, deal teams will be required to coordinate with the relevant party to obtain hard copies.

Redaction
- Some documentation, such as material correspondence, will require redaction to comply with data protection obligations.

Accessibility
- Deal teams will need to ensure that the documents are in an easily accessible format (e.g., PDF) with logical naming convention.

VDR Upload
- A VDR set up, often with one of the professional service industry's preferred platforms.
- Given the significant volume of documents, deal teams are likely to require dedicated resource for ongoing VDR management (including as new information becomes available).

IT = information technology, RM = relationship manager, VDR = virtual data room.
Source: Deloitte as cited in ADB 2022.

Smart virtual data rooms: Investors depend on both financial and nonfinancial data to conduct their due diligence. For nonfinancial data, documents often need to be manually extracted, cleaned, and organized. This process can be time-consuming, especially for portfolios with many loans. Subsequently, to provide investors secure online access, this data needs to be digitized and uploaded.

Legal and financial due diligence are traditionally the most time-consuming and costly aspect of NPL sale transactions. The unstructured data provided in VDRs need to be reviewed by qualified experts to populate missing pieces in the data template or provide qualitative summaries (roll ups) of the claim and its collateral. To date, legal and financial due diligence is largely manual. However, recent availability of powerful large language models, such as OpenAI's ChatGPT, Google's Gemini, Antropic's Claude, or Meta's Llama have revolutionized the ability of computers to understand text and complex financial or legal documents.

Some NPL transaction platforms have successfully used generative AI tools to standardize data templates and extract key values from PDF files or other documents to enrich the transaction data tape.[21]

Standard legal documents: For consistency in the sale process, some sellers use standardized internal legal templates. In Viet Nam, both VAMC and DATC use standardized debt purchase agreements but do not disclose these agreements to the public. Other international AMCs make sample sale contracts available on their websites for different asset types (e.g., KAMCO in the Republic of Korea, or Ukraine Deposit Guarantee Fund in Ukraine).

4.7 Valuation Standards from International Asset Management Companies

Valuation of assets is of great importance when AMCs acquire or sell assets. The previous sections discussed requirements for many AMCs or sellers in general in Asia and the Pacific to engage with external accredited collateral appraisers and explained the general valuation methods and data requirements. The most common reason for a failed auction is an incorrect price. The World Bank surveyed valuation methods used by several international AMCs in 2002. The three European AMCs—National Asset Management Agency in Ireland, Sareb in Spain, and Bank Assets Management Company in Slovenia—use international and, often, Royal Institute of Chartered Surveyors (RICS) valuation standards for commercial real estate valuation. National Asset Management Agency of Ireland uses market and discounted cash flow methods and follows RICS standards. The Central Bank of Spain as a regulator plays a crucial role in asset valuation practices at Sareb. All three AMCs rely on external and internal valuers to different extents (World Bank 2022).

For example, the valuation method used by Slovenia's Bank Assets Management Company includes elements of decision trees and elements of option pricing. Many loan valuation methods apply decision trees, in which each branch represents one cash flow or workout scenario, e.g., reperforming, out-of-court settlement with a discounted payoff, or judicial foreclosure of collateral. Each scenario requires assumptions about the amount and timing of the cash flows generated and the probability for each branch to occur. Valuing NPLs with option pricing methodologies is less common in practice but has the advantage to include the unknown price development of the collateral as a stochastic process with an appreciation or depreciation trend and volatility (Pelizza and Schenk-Hoppé 2020).

4.7.1 Other International Valuation Standards

The European Banking Committee has released guidance for banks on dealing with NPLs, with a particular focus on collateral valuation. The guidance offers detailed recommendations for banks to follow when valuing immovable properties held as collateral for NPLs. The key principles outlined in the guidance include the following:

(i) **Quality assurance:** This process should be carried out by a risk control unit independent of loan processing, monitoring, and underwriting. This ensures objectivity and reliability of valuation.

(ii) **Independence of external appraiser selection:** This process should be regularly tested as part of quality assurance to maintain valuation integrity.

---

[21] NPL Markets. Transforming Loan Trading with Generative AI. https://nplmarkets.com/transforming-loan-trading-with-generative-ai/.

(iii) **Regular comparison:** A representative sample of both internal and external valuations should be regularly compared against market observations to ensure accuracy.

(iv) **Back-testing:** Both internal and external collateral valuations should undergo regular back-testing to validate accuracy and reliability.

(v) **Sample size:** Quality assurance should be based on an appropriate sample size to ensure statistical significance.

The guidance puts valuation types under two categories: individual and indexed. Individual valuations are property-specific appraisals performed by an appraiser without reliance on automated processes. Indexed valuations, on the other hand, are based on indexation or automated methods and can be used to update valuations for certain cases.

Appraisers, whether internal or external, need to be qualified, possess relevant experience, and execute valuations independently. Banks should maintain an approved panel of such appraisers and assess their performance over time. The independence of appraisers is crucial, and the guidelines outline several criteria for independence, including not being involved in loan processing or credit decisions, avoiding conflicts of interest, maintaining impartiality, and providing objective valuation reports.

Frequent valuations are recommended, with individual valuations for collateral needing updates at least annually for commercial immovable properties and every 3 years for residential properties.

The guidance also highlights that immovable property collateral should be valued based on market value or mortgage lending value, and overall valuations solely based on discounted replacement cost are discouraged. For income-generating properties, market comparable or discounted cash flow approaches are suitable.

In summary, the European Banking Committee's guidance provides comprehensive recommendations for banks to follow when valuing immovable property collateral for NPLs, focusing on independence, regular assessments, and appropriate valuation methodologies based on market observations.

Royal Institution of Chartered Surveyors valuation standards: Many countries publish guidelines on the valuation of real estate. Internationally well-known are the guidelines from the RICS, which provide comprehensive guidelines for valuing real estate properties. These guidelines ensure consistent and professional valuation practices in the real estate industry.[22]

4.7.2 Valuation Haircuts in Judicial Auctions

This study emphasizes the importance of "purpose" for valuing NPLs. A piece of real estate collateral sold at judicial auction will very likely not attract the open market value for the property. Hence, NPL practitioners focus on the liquidation value at which the property can be sold at auction. The haircut to open market value can be as high as 65% for illiquid industrial properties, reducing to less than 10% for desirable residential properties. Many reasons explain the liquidation haircut in judicial auctions. Platforms that offer judicial auctions may want to address these points to achieve better outcomes. Real estate sold at judicial auctions often sell for less than their open market value due to a combination of legal, financial, and market factors:

---

[22]   RICS. https://www.rics.org/profession-standards/rics-standards-and-guidance/sector-standards/valuation-standards.

(i) **Distressed condition:** Properties undergoing foreclosure may be in poor physical condition due to neglect or lack of maintenance by the distressed owner. Buyers may factor in the cost of repairs and renovations, leading to lower bids.

(ii) **Limited market exposure:** Judicial auctions typically have a limited audience of potential buyers, mainly investors or individuals seeking bargains. The stigma associated with foreclosure properties can lead to negative perceptions and lower perceived value among potential buyers. This contrasts with the broader exposure that properties listed on the open market receive, which can attract a wider range of buyers.

(iii) **Time constraints:** Foreclosure can be time-consuming and unpredictable. Auctions often have strict timelines, which can lead to rushed sales.

(iv) **Lack of financing:** Auction sales often require immediate payment in cash or a substantial deposit. Buyers who rely on mortgage financing might be excluded from participating.

(v) **Lack of information:** Buyers at foreclosure auctions might have limited access to property information, making it harder for them to accurately assess the value of the property.

(vi) **Bidding dynamics:** The auction environment can be competitive, leading to rapid bidding that might not reflect the true market value of the property. This dynamic can result in properties being sold for less than their open market value.

While properties sold at judicial auctions may often sell for less than their open market value, this is not always the case. Factors such as location, property condition, market demand, and the level of competition among bidders will influence the final sale price.

In summary, standardized data templates help market participants understand the important data requirement in an NPL transaction. Standard templates will only help the market to become more efficient if their use is widespread or mandatory. Sellers know that a certain minimum information set is required from them, and buyers can easily understand and automatically process and value loan portfolios based on standardized data, making a successful sale more likely and faster to execute. For complex loans or assets, the data tape—even if comprehensive and of good quality—will not in itself be sufficient to execute a trade. Investors need to conduct detailed legal and financial due diligence, requiring access to unstructured information outside the data tapes typically provided in a VDR. The emerging use of generative AI will help accelerate legal and financial due diligence processes referred to as smart VDRs. The NPL valuation can be complex and some NPL transaction platforms provide powerful self-service valuation tools (Figure 13).

4.8 Data Warehousing and Data Hub Function of Nonperforming Loan Platforms

The accurate valuation of NPLs requires either a large dataset of comparable prices for a mark-to-market valuation or many model parameters to generate the future cash flows for a discounted cash flow analysis (mark-to-model). Often, NPLs are illiquid, and a suitable market is not available, leaving the model-based valuation the most common alternative. An online transaction platform can operate as a data warehouse for loan and collateral data, market prices, and actual cash flow data. If such information is made available to all market participants for valuation and benchmarking, then such a data warehouse is referred to as a "data hub." A data hub will make valuation of loans easier and more reliable and reduce the risk that transactions fail due to insurmountable bid–offer spreads.

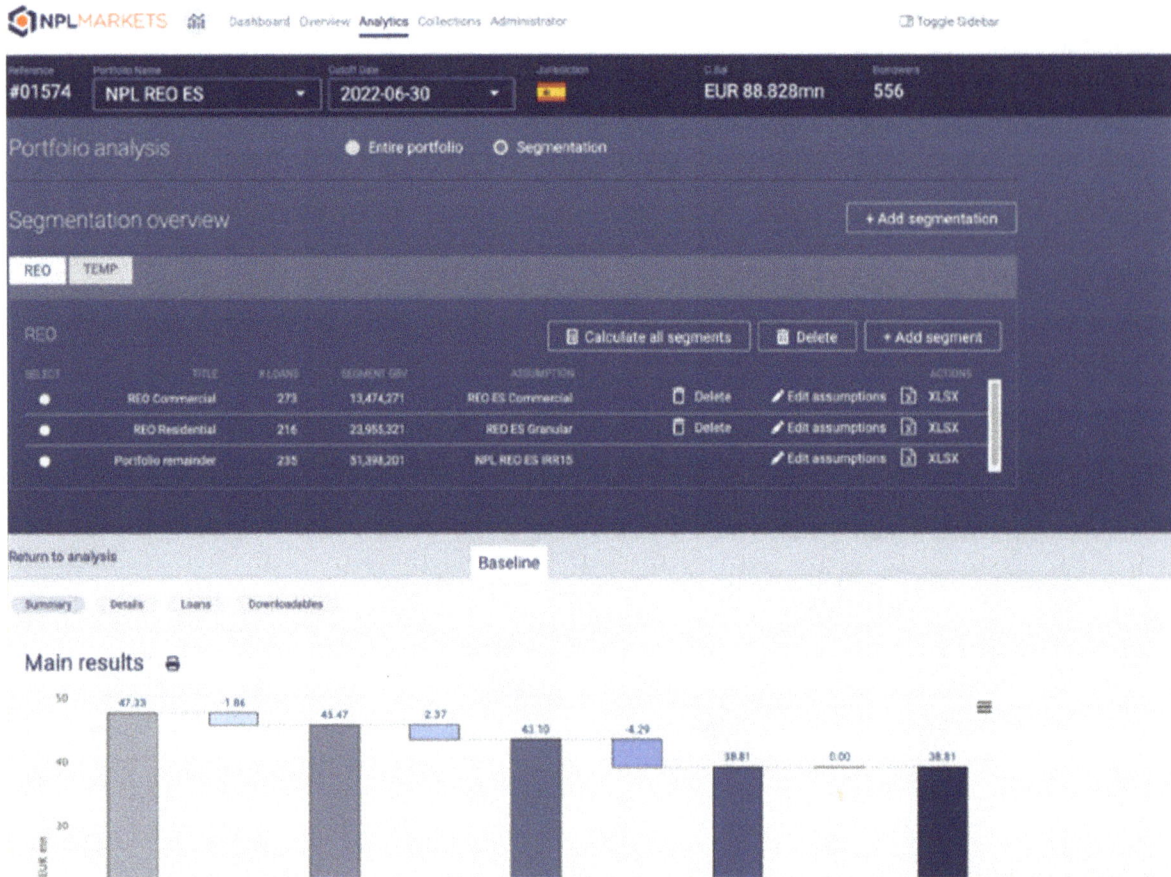

Figure 13: Loan Validation and Segmentation Tool

Source: nplmarkets.com.

The data hub can exist separately from the platform and its transaction execution and auction functions and may even be organized outside of the platform as part of a publicly owned or publicly sponsored central data repository. The proposal to have a central data exchange in Kazakhstan has been discussed in Chapter 2, and, in Europe, central data repositories exist for securitization data and are being discussed for NPL transaction and NPL performance data as well. To overcome a lack of transparency of NPL recovery cash flows and market prices it is essential that market participants can see the price of an asset sold at auction, as well as see the exact characteristics of the assets sold (where the identity of the borrowers and individuals is suitably kept anonymous).

When designing a data hub function, it is critical to decide which data is made available to all market participants and whether to mandate the delivery of information to the data hub through suitable legislation. Data hubs that rely on voluntary deliveries are unlikely to gather a critical mass of information. At a minimum, the data should be available based on a detailed standardized data tape and the achieved market price.

Securitization data repositories report the detailed cash flows and change in outstanding balances on regular reporting quarters (typically monthly or quarterly).[23] A central repository for loan-by-loan, period-by-period recovery cash flows would be a powerful tool to help sellers and buyers better price their claims and assets. Examples exists of privately organized recovery data repositories supported by large international financial institutions that operate on a voluntary basis, but their coverage and use in Asia and the Pacific is limited.[24]

What type of information should a data hub function of an NPL transaction platform collect that has the biggest impact on the market? The answer is any data that directly helps investors to price NPLs more accurately or that helps identify the most suitable buyers for the NPLs on offer.

(i)   Loan-level transaction data of the prices at which NPL or assets traded including a description of the assets.

(ii) Loan-level cash flow performance data tracking loan, borrower, and collateral information, together with the actual cash flows received by the lender (loan data tapes with historical collections). In the US, the large mortgage agencies Fannie Mae and Freddy Mac have published loan-level performance data for millions of residential mortgages for over 20 years. In Europe a large portion of the loan-level data from securitization transactions is centrally collected in a small number of accredited data repositories collecting detailed performance histories on millions of loans over many years covering different macroeconomic environments.

(iii) Investor profiles and preferences capturing the contact details, past investment and bidding behavior, and investment guidelines or preferences from institutional investors.

(iv) Aggregated performance data that show statistical averages for different loans, borrowers, and collateral clusters for recovery rates, average time to recovery, and cost of recovery. This data often exists in central credit registers such as the Credit Information Center in Viet Nam, in the Anacredit database of the European Central Bank. An example of such recovery statistics from the Bank of Italy is shown in Table 5.

Table 5: Recovery Rates by Secured Status, Year of Resolution, and Default Vintage

Years		Secured by Collateral		Unsecured	
Year of closure	Vintage	Amount (€ million)	Recovery Rate (%)	Amount (€ million)	Recovery Rate (%)
2022	0–2 years	459	67.4	427	54.5
	3–5 years	653	55.3	325	43.1
	>5 years	1,497	42.6	798	34.0
	Total	**2,609**	**50.1**	**1,549**	**41.5**
2021	0–2 years	539	64.8	413	40.0
	3–5 years	630	57.7	302	41.2
	>5 years	1,308	40.7	727	28.6
	Total	**2,477**	**50.3**	**1,442**	**34.5**

continued on next page

---

[23] For example, the European Data Warehouse, eurodw.eu, collects data from standardized investor disclosures for securitization transactions.

[24] Such as Global Credit Data, which is a not-for-profit association of international banks, at globalcreditdata.com. It collects wholesale historical loan recovery data from member banks.

Table 5 *continued*

Years		Secured by Collateral		Unsecured	
Year of closure	Vintage	Amount (€ million)	Recovery Rate (%)	Amount (€ million)	Recovery Rate (%)
2020	0–2 years	741	64.0	648	50.2
	3–5 years	895	51.8	512	46.2
	>5 years	1,937	41.0	1,014	27.9
	Total	**3,572**	**48.5**	**2,173**	**38.0**
2019	0–2 years	996	61.2	648	46.6
	3–5 years	1,506	52.6	512	33.3
	>5 years	2,174	38.8	1,014	28.4
	Total	**4,675**	**48.0**	**2,173**	**35.0**
2018	0–2 years	1,625	63.5	1,071	44.8
	3–5 years	1,963	57.9	974	40.4
	>5 years	2,844	42.4	2,317	30.3
	Total	**6,432**	**52.4**	**4,363**	**36.1**
2017	0–2 years	1,529	68.5	1,196	40.6
	3–5 years	1,546	59.3	1,108	31.7
	>5 years	2,760	44.2	2,210	25.4
	Total	**5,834**	**54.6**	**4,515**	**31.0**
2016	0–2 years	1,375	68.9	1,144	45.4
	3–5 years	1,271	54.5	1,044	34.6
	>5 years	2,193	43.5	2,127	24.0
	Total	**4,840**	**53.6**	**4,315**	**32.2**

Source: Fischetto et al. 2022 based on Central Credit Register of the Bank of Italy.

Such data is regularly published in central bank reports like semi-annual financial stability reports. Unfortunately, however, these aggregated disclosures are not optimally designed for NPL market participants. High level recovery rates may be published (Table 5), but there is less specific information on the timing and cost of recoveries. A very useful publication was conducted by EBA as a judicial benchmark study across many countries and asset classes. Unfortunately, this insight was provided at one time only and has not since been repeated. The World Bank published their Doing Business database until 2020, which included data on enforcement and insolvency processes in many countries.

The screenshot in Figure 14 shows an online data warehouse example from the European DataWarehouse. Many filter options are available to find the required datasets. Datasets include loan level performance data and transactions documents from European securitization transactions.

Figure 14: Central Public Data Repository for Loan Portfolio Performance Data

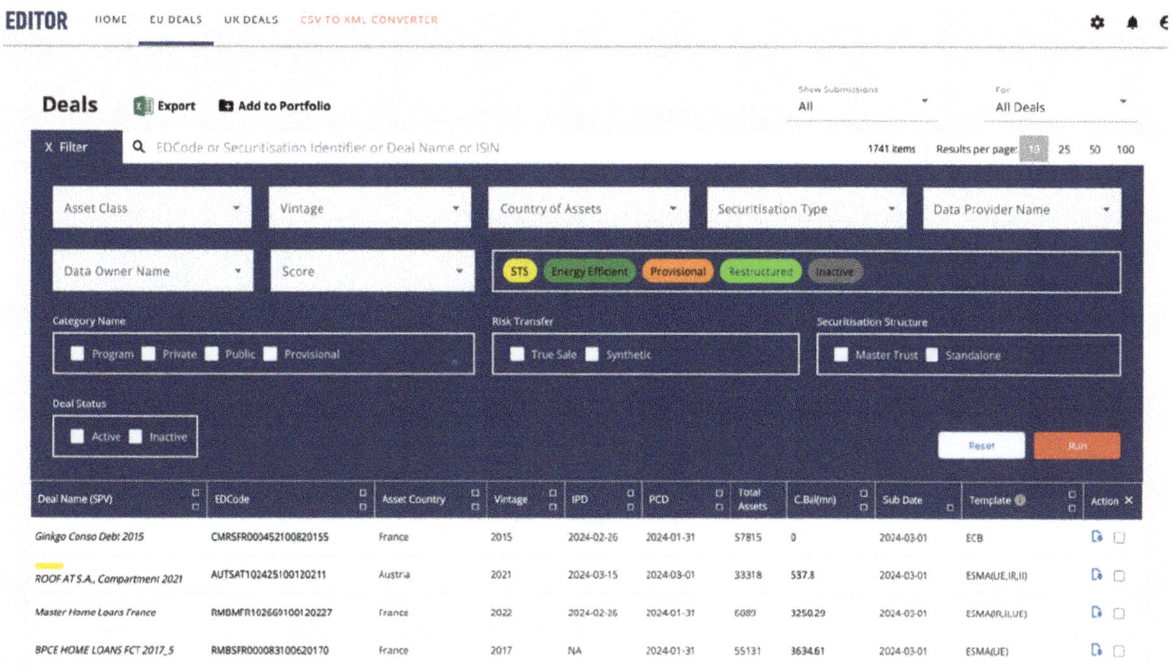

Source: European DataWarehouse. www.eurodw.eu.

5 Blueprint for Nonperforming Loan Trading Platforms

This chapter provides a high-level blueprint for the establishment of a new NPL transaction platform in Asia and the Pacific. The chapter draws practical considerations based on experience in setting up NPL trading platforms in many jurisdictions, mostly in Europe, from the European Bank for Reconstruction and Development feasibility study on regulating an NPL trading platform in Kazakhstan (KPMG 2023), and the road map report of the first feasibility study by ADB.

5.1 Platform Types and Business Models

Three types of platforms are considered to differentiate their regulatory regimes and operational demands. These may be integrated into a single platform or co-exist as different legal entities:

(i)   **Information platforms:** Information platforms connect buyers and sellers online, facilitate transactions through auction functions to determine winning bidder(s), and provide ancillary services such as data preparation and valuation tools or virtual data rooms to support due diligence. Most business-to-business (B2B) NPL platforms that focus on institutional sales fall into this category. They do not take client money and do not settle transactions.

(ii) **Trading systems:** Multilateral trading facilities or alternative trading systems fall into this category as do consumer-focused business-to-consumer (B2C) auction platforms that handle the payments and settlement of the assets sold. Trading systems are subject to additional regulations compared to information platforms and may include some or all the functions of information platforms.

(iii) **Data hubs:** The data warehouse function can be an integrated part of information platforms or trading systems. The data hub can also be separated from transaction functions for two reasons: first, the data hub follows a different business model from transaction platforms. The hubs do not connect buyers and sellers and do not run auctions. As a data service their user fees are not conditional on the successful closing of a transaction. Second, there is a case to be made for specific regulations and public sector interventions to create a central data hub as a market utility, even in markets where NPL trading is advanced and NPL trading platforms exist.

Single function versus multifunction platforms: Other platform classifications exist based on their key activities. Marketplace platforms focus on offering assets with few ancillary services. Auction platforms offer assets and conduct auctions (often used for judicial auctions and enforcement sales). Valuation platforms focus on valuation services without the obligation to trade on the platform. Multifunctional platforms provide all or most of the possible services: data preparation, data hub, valuation, reporting and marketplace with transaction and due diligence advice.

Asset perimeter: Some platforms focus on (mostly unsecured) retail NPL portfolios connecting banks with debt collection agencies. Some platforms focus on corporate NPLs only. Auction platforms mostly focus on asset sales including residential real estate and movable assets. The most generalist platforms support retail and corporate portfolios of secured and unsecured claims, foreclosed assets (real estate-owned), and loans with different performance states, i.e., performing, sub-performing and nonperforming.

Geographic reach: The strategic geographical scope of transaction platforms holds the potential to optimize transactional efficiency and expand market reach, thereby capitalizing on economies of scale. This suggests that, particularly for smaller markets, the ideal objective should be to establish a platform capable of facilitating regional transactions. By doing so, sellers dealing with NPLs in less prominent markets could enhance their appeal to investors.

ADB's first feasibility study explained in detail that NPL markets in Asia and the Pacific vary in their developmental stages across jurisdictions, with some countries necessitating substantial legal reforms to attract investors and foster a functional market, including enhancements in collateral enforcement and asset ownership. Consequently, the progression toward a regional platform should be executed incrementally, with an initial focus on countries well-prepared for the transition, followed by the inclusion of other countries as they become ready. However, this sequential approach should not hinder individual countries from establishing their own domestic platforms.

The objective here is to create a blueprint for platforms that start their operation in one domestic market and then expand their activities by supporting cross-border investments dealing with domestic and international investors. This study also recommends adjustments of the operations of existing NPL platforms to support best practice transaction processes.

5.1.1 Typical Fee Elements for Existing Platforms

Fees charged by platforms vary by type of business model and need to be set at a level that makes commercial sense for the platform operator, i.e., cover operational and capital expenses plus an attractive return to shareholders. Fee structures should be transparent and levels affordable to users regardless of size so as not to act as a disincentive to smaller buyers or sellers. Ultimately, low fee levels are only possible with a critical mass of users.

- **Registration fee:** Buyer registration is generally free of charge to encourage participation, but some platforms charge a registration fee.

- **Listing fee:** The seller may pay for listing the single asset or portfolio on the platform. However, some institutional platforms do not charge for listing and require a success fee only.

- **Transaction fee:** To be paid in case a bid is accepted by the seller. This fee can be payable regardless of whether the deal is completed or is conditional on completion.

- **Data preparation fee:** Paid by the seller and depends on the scope of transaction preparation work, portfolio selection, and data validation work required from the platform.

- **Virtual data room fees:** Some institutional sellers prefer to use their own approved VDR technology especially for larger portfolio sales. If a specific third party VDR is required, then the use of the VDR may incur an additional fee.

- **Cybersecurity fees:** Some sellers have specific cybersecurity requirements that may incur an additional fee. For example, a single sign on functions or user supplied encryption keys may incur an additional charge.

- **Software-as-a-service subscription fees:** Sellers who want to insource platform software tools using a SaaS agreement will be charged an annual subscription fee plus an initial set up fee.

Fee levels vary by the size of the assets sold and increase the more value-added services the seller or buyer requires. Listing fees tend to be modest and can start at $100 per item listed. Success-based transaction fees can start at $5,000, or 2% to 3% of the sales price for smaller tickets. Larger portfolio transaction fees can be in the range of 0.5% to 1% of the sale price. Annual platform SaaS subscription fees can start at $10,000 whereas larger banks selling more frequently should expect to pay at least $50,000. These numbers are indicative for some internationally active platforms. NPL sales processes, especially for portfolios, tend to be bespoke with individually negotiated service levels.

5.2 Benefits for Sellers and Buyers in Nonperforming Loan Transaction Platforms

The creation of electronic platforms for distressed asset trading offers various options and considerations to expand the market and provide efficient mechanisms for NPL transactions (Figure 15). These platforms serve as marketplaces where banks can sell NPLs following standardized processes, reaching a wider range of investors, including unconventional participants. The platforms enhance market accessibility for international investors by providing structured and unstructured data on assets for sale, while adhering to regulatory and legislative constraints. Unlike AMCs, these platforms are market-oriented solutions and do not own the assets.

Chapter 1 reviews the general principles, the key features, and business practices. Comprehensive online NPL trading platforms encompass end-to-end process management covering the entire NPL sales process, from asset selection, data preparation, contract negotiations, VDR due diligence services, to final sale, covering various related business processes. Data hubs facilitate data exchange with real-time relational data warehouses, virtual data rooms and automatic data validation, allowing potential buyers to review information about assets, transaction prices, market insights and historical performance data. Auction functionality with customizable parameters, such as auction type, price limits, and auction steps, is often provided. Platforms offer ancillary services like transaction advice, asset marketing, valuation, reporting, and due diligence support.

Benefits for sellers:

- Efficient market access, even for small portfolios; low transaction costs; fair and transparent pricing; full auditable transaction record of all investor interactions; and access to advisory services and third-party service providers.

- NPL transaction platforms offer potentially significant process benefits to users, including wider and deeper channels to market and better matching between buyers and sellers.

- Platforms provide access to a large investor base and access to new investors who would not have been known to the seller prior to starting the sales process.

- Anecdotally, platforms offer faster execution with a 50% or larger time saving over traditional processes.

- Lower transaction costs, again, at least a 50% saving on traditional advisory services and better pricing with price improvements of 20% to 30% having been observed in like-for-like repeat institutional transactions between traditional and platform processes.

Advantages for buyers:

- Safe environment for purchasing NPLs with streamlined onboarding processes, document exchanges, transparent and standardized information, well organized processes with clear timelines and support, real time notifications of any process changes, and communication tools with the seller, the platform, or advisors.

- The platform provides process oversight by an independent third party, eases the interaction with third-party service providers, helps establish relationships with loan servicers, and can help with the arrangements of financing for the buyers of large portfolios.

- Eligible buyers participate in auctions in line with legal limitations.

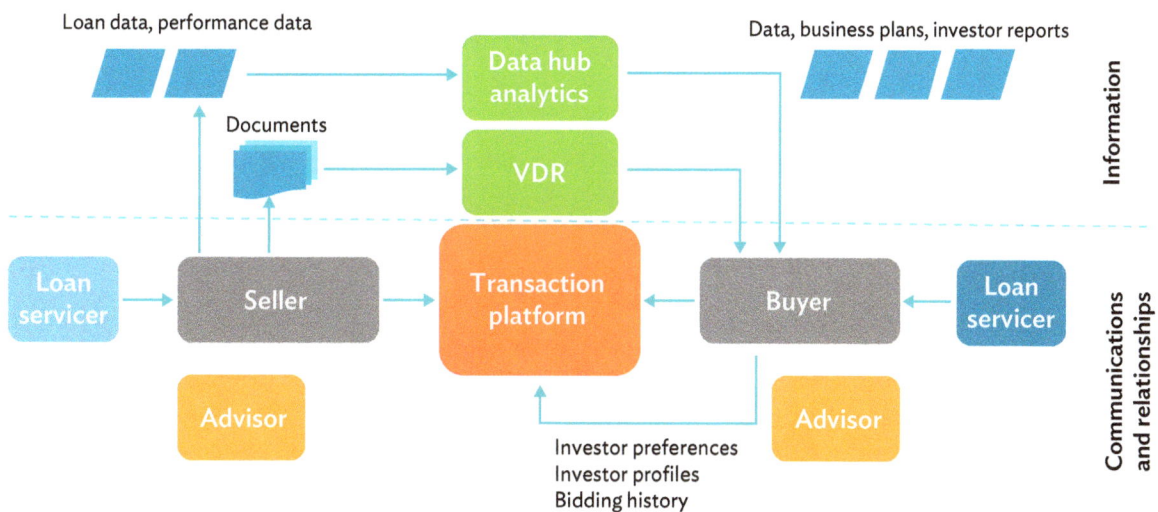

Figure 15: Intermediation of Buyers and Sellers by a Transaction Platform Including the Exchange of Structured and Unstructured Data for Valuation and Due Diligence

VDR = virtual data room.
Source: nplmarkets.com.

5.3 Supervisory Incentives to Use Nonperforming Loan Trading Platforms

The benefits listed above provide the general incentive for market participants to use NPL platforms including wider and deeper channels to market, faster execution of deals, lower transactional costs, better pricing, and higher transparency of disposal process. Despite the many benefits of using online platforms, the majority of large institutional NPL sales are still done offline through traditional processes. Repeat sellers may be reluctant to change their established processes with their existing advisors and counterparties and as mentioned above, the benefits of using online platforms may be hard to quantify. Supervisors who want to improve market efficiency, transparency, and the use of platforms have several options to consider:

- A potential mandatory use of transaction platforms could vastly increase online trading activities (see the example of Kazakhstan in Chapter 2).

- The use of standard data template could be made mandatory (see the example of the European or Kazakhstan data templates in Chapter 4).

- The delivery of transaction data to a central data hub for improved market transparency and supervisory monitoring could be mandated (see the example from the European securitization market in Chapter 4).

Bank supervisors can offer various incentives to encourage banks to actively trade their NPLs including the use of NPL trading platforms and data hubs and thereby promoting the health of financial systems.

(i) **Regulatory capital relief:** Supervisors can provide such relief to banks on their stock of NPLs if those banks demonstrate through the delivery of information to a data hub or through their NPL sales activities that the value of the assets materially exceeds the net book values imposed by supervisors. Many countries have rules that force banks to create additional provisions or use capital add-ons for NPLs that have not been resolved within a certain time limit. If the bank could demonstrate through trading or data deliveries that certain minimum recoveries are likely, then capital charges could be reduced, and the banks are incentivized to establish valuation benchmarks using platforms or data hubs.

(ii) **Performance-based incentives:** Introducing performance-based incentives tied to NPL reduction targets can motivate banks to trade NPLs. Supervisors could reward banks that achieve specific reduction goals through trading activities. Examples include requirements for banks that exceed the NPL ratio threshold to come up with detailed NPL reduction plans. Banks that use platforms and data hubs but breach the NPL ratio threshold could be granted leniency from creating such NPL reduction plans.

(iii) **Enhanced reporting and data sharing:** Supervisors can provide additional data on NPL market trends, helping banks make informed decisions about trading. Improved data sharing can create a more transparent and competitive market. Many supervisors require banks to report the details of any NPL transaction sale or securitization transaction. If these reports are only accessible by supervisors, then there is no benefit to other market participants. Sharing anonymous reports with publicly accessible data hubs would increase transparency and reduce the barrier for new investors to enter the market.

These incentives, tailored to the specific needs and challenges of individual countries, can collectively drive a more dynamic NPL trading market, benefiting both financial institutions and the broader economy.

5.4 Success Factors for Establishing a Nonperforming Loan Trading Platform

Setting up a new NPL platform involves careful planning, adherence to regulations, and the creation of a supportive infrastructure. Following are key success factors for establishing a successful NPL platform:

(i) **Market structure design and eligible assets:** Designing a well-structured marketplace that meets the needs of participants. This includes determining the types of loans, claims, and assets to be traded, trading mechanisms, pricing methods, and transparency rules. Consumer-focused asset auction platforms may not be well-equipped to deal with complex portfolio transactions. Institutional platforms typically do not have a large user base of private individuals for smaller asset sales.

(ii) **Technology infrastructure:** Building a robust and scalable technology platform that can handle trading volumes, execute transactions efficiently, and provide real-time market data. Developing an intuitive and user-friendly trading interface that caters to either institutional or retail investors or both. The platform should be accessible and easy to navigate. Providing easy access to market participants, including investors, brokers, loan services, and other service providers. Clear onboarding processes and connectivity options are essential.

(iii) **Transparency and reporting:** Implementing transparent transaction rules and providing timely and accurate market data. Transparency enhances investor confidence and encourages participation. Establishing procedures for uploading and showcasing (listing) of transactions on the platform and maintaining relationships with banks, AMCs, and other sellers is important. Clear data requirements and a streamlined listing process are important for attracting new sellers.

(iv) **Investor protection:** Implementing measures to protect investors' interests, including to prevent conflicts of interest, ensuring fair treatment of all participants, and providing investor education. Developing and using comprehensive transaction procedures and process guidelines. These documents provide clarity to market participants about how the NPL platform operates.

(v) **Payment and settlement (if applicable):** A well-functioning payment and settlement process is crucial for minimizing counterparty risk. Safeguarding deposits from potential buyers and returning those to unsuccessful bidders in a timely manner.

(vi) **Marketing and promotion:** Attract market participants and raise awareness about the NPL platform. Effective marketing helps build a strong participant base both for sellers and buyers. In most markets, listing NPLs for sale on a website or platform alone will not likely attract the interest of the most suitable buyers. Institutional investors may scan the platform from time to time for opportunities but would still expect to be contacted directly if a suitable transaction enters the market.

(vii) **Continuous innovation and collaboration:** Being open to innovation and adapting to changing market dynamics. Regularly updating and enhancing the NPL platform based on industry trends and feedback from market participants. Collaborate with industry stakeholders, including regulators, market participants, and technology providers. Strong collaboration ensures a supportive ecosystem for the platform.

Successful platform development requires a comprehensive approach that addresses regulatory, technological, operational, and market-related considerations. By carefully addressing these key success factors, NPL platform operators can create a well-functioning and competitive trading platform that attracts market participants and contributes to overall market development.

5.5 Regulatory Compliance of Nonperforming Loan Transaction Platforms

Regulatory compliance is a critical aspect of operating a transaction platform to ensure fair and transparent trading, investor protection, and market integrity. The specific legal and regulatory requirements in Viet Nam and the Republic of Korea were discussed in Chapter 3. The following regulatory compliance issues are important for NPL transaction platforms in any country:

(i)   **Licensing and registration:** Obtain the necessary licenses, approvals, or registrations from the relevant regulatory authorities to operate as an NPL Platform. This may involve compliance with banking laws, trading regulations, and other financial industry regulations.

(ii) **Market regulations:** Adhere to the specific market regulations that govern platform operations especially platforms operating as trading venues or trading systems (see above, information platforms are unlikely to fall under the market regulation that applies to trading venues). Auction platforms can be subject to rules related to trading hours, order types, transparency, reporting, and price discovery mechanisms.

(iii) **Transparency, reporting, and notifications:** Maintain transparency by providing real-time market data, trade reporting, and disclosure of information to the public. Accurate and timely reporting helps investors make informed decisions. Fulfill reporting obligations to regulatory authorities, including trade reporting, data submission, and periodic reporting. Timely and accurate reporting is crucial for regulatory oversight.

(iv) **Recordkeeping and audit trails:** Maintain comprehensive records of all trading activities, including binding offers, executions, cancellations, and amendments. These records should be easily accessible for regulatory audits.

(v)   **Anti-money laundering and know your customer:** Implement AML and KYC procedures to verify the identity of participants. Conduct due diligence with potential participants to ensure they meet the required standards. Monitor transactions for suspicious activities and report any suspicious transactions to relevant authorities.

(vi) **Cybersecurity:** Implement robust cybersecurity measures to protect the platform, participant data, and trading information from cyber threats. This includes data security and encryption, access controls, regular penetration tests, disaster recovery and incident response plans.

(vii) **Data privacy:** Ensure compliance with data protection and privacy regulations. Safeguard participant information and ensure that data is collected, processed, and stored in accordance with applicable laws.

(viii) **Risk management:** Develop and implement risk management protocols to manage operational, technical, and financial risks. Have procedures for handling trading disruptions, system failures, and other contingencies.

By addressing these regulatory compliance issues, NPL platform operators can establish a secure and compliant trading environment that fosters trust among participants and contributes to the overall health of the financial markets.

5.6 Governance and Ownership of Nonperforming Loan Transaction Platforms

Facilitating a cross-border transaction market requires collaborative effort and universally accepted minimum standards across the region. International development institutions such as ADB or the World Bank can play a pivotal role as standard setters. These organizations could help define and institute common standards that govern cross-border transactions. Complying with these standards would give the platform a prestigious "seal of approval," which has the potential to bolster user confidence significantly.

Alternatively, an industry-wide independent standard setter within the region is a viable approach. By leveraging existing industry entities like the IPAF, establishment of unified standards could be expedited, enhancing the integrity and credibility of the cross-border transaction market.

To operate effectively, platforms must adhere to national laws and regulations in their jurisdictions. Like existing institutional platforms, an information platform would not engage in settlement services or participate in legal contracting. Instead, these functions would occur offline through bilateral agreements between involved parties. Additionally, the platform would not hold ownership of the assets in question. And by regulatory classification, the platforms would not qualify as financial market infrastructure and typically would not fall under regulatory oversight.

(i)   **Ownership and control:** Clearly define the ownership structure of the platform and the roles of key stakeholders, including shareholders, operators, and participants. Avoid conflicts of interest that could compromise the platform's integrity. This is particularly relevant where the platform is owned by the same or related entity acting as seller. As noted, platforms can be owned and operated by dedicated entities that built the platform internally, own all the intellectual property, and are generally in full control of the operations. However, hybrid models may be more cost-efficient where the entire platform operation or selected features like VDRs or valuation tools are insourced from external parties. In this case, detailed service level agreements are required to agree control issues, operational issues, help desks, and risk management procedures.

(ii) **Board of directors:** Establish a board of directors with diverse expertise to provide oversight, strategic direction, and decision-making. Independent directors can enhance transparency and prevent undue influence. Platforms operating as market utilities and data hubs benefit from independent directors representing the interests of all market participants.

(iii) **Operational independence and integrity:** Ensure the NPL platform operates independently of any single market participant or owner to prevent favoritism or bias. This independence is crucial for fair execution and investor trust. Develop policies and mechanisms to identify, manage, and disclose conflicts of interest among operators, participants, and owners. Transparency in managing conflicts is essential. Prioritize market integrity and ensure the platform maintains a level playing field for all participants. Prevent market manipulation, insider trading, and other unfair practices.

(iv) **Rules and governance framework:** Develop and implement comprehensive rules and governance policies that outline trading procedures, membership criteria and terms of use, bidding procedures, fee structures, and dispute resolution mechanisms.

(v)   **Transparency and disclosure:** Provide clear information to participants and the public about the NPL platform's operations, rules, fees, and execution practices. Regularly update participants about changes and enhancements. Provide fair and equal access to market data for all participants. Avoid discriminatory practices that could give information advantages to some participants.

(vi) **Risk management:** Establish a comprehensive risk management framework to identify, assess, and mitigate risks associated with trading, operations, technology, and market disruptions. Ensure the platform's technological infrastructure is reliable, secure, and capable of handling high trading volumes. Implement disaster recovery and business continuity plans.

(vii) **Ongoing review and improvement:** Regularly review and assess the NPL platform's governance framework, rules, and operational procedures and improve them as challenges and market developments emerge.

By addressing these governance issues, NPL platform operators can create a well-regulated and transparent trading environment that promotes investor confidence, market integrity, and fair competition.

5.7 Operational Details of Core and Ancillary Services

Existing debt trading platforms routinely provide a comprehensive list of core and additional services to support debt sales. Core services include the upload of transaction details on the platform, showcasing (listing) of assets for sale, connecting sellers and buyers, inviting investors from an existing investor base or investors registering their interest online. Platforms facilitate transaction execution through competitive bidding in auctions of different types. The platform plays an important role in the successful execution of NPL transactions by fully displaying NPL details, managing transaction timing and process, organizing due diligence and auctions, and generally helping communication and negotiations between buyers and sellers.

Activities of sellers: Sellers using NPL platforms are credit institutions or nonbank lenders that sell loans they originated in the so-called primary market. Secondary market sellers are AMCs, loan servicers, debt collectors, or institutional investors who have acquired loans in the primary market and now wish to sell parts of the assets they acquired. Tertiary market transactions exist but are less common. In this case, investors or securitization vehicles who acquired NPLs in the secondary market may sell down assets to other investors.

After selecting a suitable platform, sellers register on the platform and sign an engagement letter with the platform operator. Sellers provide information regarding assets offered for sale, including loan data tapes in the form of standard data templates. Sellers provide additional unstructured information for due diligence and at the request of interested potential investors. Sellers decide whether to use the platform legal documents for nondisclosure agreements, process letters, teasers, sale and purchase agreements, and any other marketing information or whether they prefer to provide their own approved documents. Sellers decide the marketing strategy, including which investors to invite to the transaction process and what information to disclose to the public via the listing prior to signing nondisclosure agreements.

Sellers may require advisory support on which assets to select from a larger perimeter of assets and with the creation of standardized loan data tapes. For high-value assets, sellers may conduct a sell-side due diligence and valuation to understand the market price for the distressed assets offered for sale. Sellers may need to assist the due diligence process by providing answers to the questions from investors. Sellers need to agree with the transaction process which includes the decision about running an initial nonbinding offer phase or a single binding offer phase only. The binding offer can be run as closed bid tenders or open bid timed auctions or a combination of different methods in multiple bidding rounds. Eventually, the seller signs the loan sale and purchase and accompanying documents with the winning bidder(s) based on the prices bid on the platform and pays fees to the platform operator. Before or after closing of an NPL transaction, the seller notifies the borrowers of the sale.

Activities of buyers: Buyers may be private individuals for foreclosed assets or institutional investors for loan portfolios sales. Institutional investors can be AMCs, debt funds, debt trading companies, debt collection agencies, loan servicing companies or other commercial or investment banks. Buyers register on the platform and analyze data uploaded by the seller and decide whether to participate in the sales process and sign nondisclosure agreements with the seller. Participating investors are granted access to the VDR to conduct due diligence and valuation and participate in the auction. The winning buyer will sign the sales and purchase agreements, pay the purchase price, and take over the assets in the agreed settlement process.

User registration: The registration process should be formalized and should not include any discriminative provisions such as obligation to establish a legal presence or any obligations in terms of organizational form of entities that submit for registration. Advanced platforms provide an online onboarding user interface and process. Users provide contact and organizational details, electronically sign the required terms of use and other registration documents like data processing agreements, and upload any supporting documents required for KYC, AML, sanction checks, licenses, etc. Investors can specify their preferences and investment experience and provide a company presentation showing their investment expertise and track record to encourage sellers to invite them to a transaction process.

Investor profiling and marketing: Platforms often have a large database of institutional investors with their company profiles and investment preferences. The platform's service to profile and vet investor helps with targeting the most suitable investors and accelerates the advertising and marketing process of a sales transaction. B2C platforms list the assets for sale and let the investors register their interest in participating in the sale or auction. Listing websites are well-known from e-commerce auction platforms like eBay or Taobao or residential property listing services like Zillow or Rightmove. B2B platforms may also list their deals publicly or announce transactions to suitable institutional investors only. The institutional investors are identified by the platform by matching the trade with the preferences stated in the investor database or by letting the seller select investors to be invited to the transaction.

Asset showcasing: The listing function and website is an essential part of B2C platforms and is often used by B2B platforms as well. Some platforms require registration before the user can see the listed transactions. For large transactions, financial institutions may not wish to announce their transactions publicly in advance and large institutional investors are used to being contacted about transactions directly rather than searching for deals on listing websites. Institutional platforms focusing on portfolio sales may not have many transactions for sale at any one point in time. In contrast, large B2C platforms may list hundreds of thousands of assets. Figure 16 shows an example of institutional listing websites from the PRC's 360pai.com. The key technical and operational features of the showcase function are as follows:

- User-friendly interface: Easy-to-navigate interface for property search and interaction.
- Search filters: Advanced filters for precise deal searches.
- User interest: Button for user to register their interest in the deal.
- Summary listings: Short deal descriptions with images and pin on the map. Auction timing.
- Detailed deal description/teaser: Detailed presentation of the assets and the transaction.
- Interactive maps: Property locations and nearby amenities displayed on maps.
- Mobile responsiveness: Seamless experience across devices.
- Messaging system: In-platform chat for user communication.
- Real-time notifications: Alerts for new listings and updates.

- Secure payment gateways: Safe transaction processing (if applicable).

- Asset classes and property categories: Categorization of residential, commercial, land, etc.

- Seller profiles: Detailed profiles for sellers and agents.

- Listing management: Editing, updates, and views tracking.

- Reviews and ratings: User feedback and trust-building reviews.

- Saved searches: Alerts for new assets matching saved criteria.

- Legal guidance: Information on legal procedures and documentation.

- Agent/broker tools: Features for managing multiple listings and clients and bulk uploads.

- Customer support: Access to assistance, frequently asked questions, and resources.

These listing features collectively enhance the platform's usability, facilitate transactions, and create a seamless experience for users engaging with the platform.

Figure 16: Screenshot of Asset Listings on Selected Nonperforming Loan Trading Platform

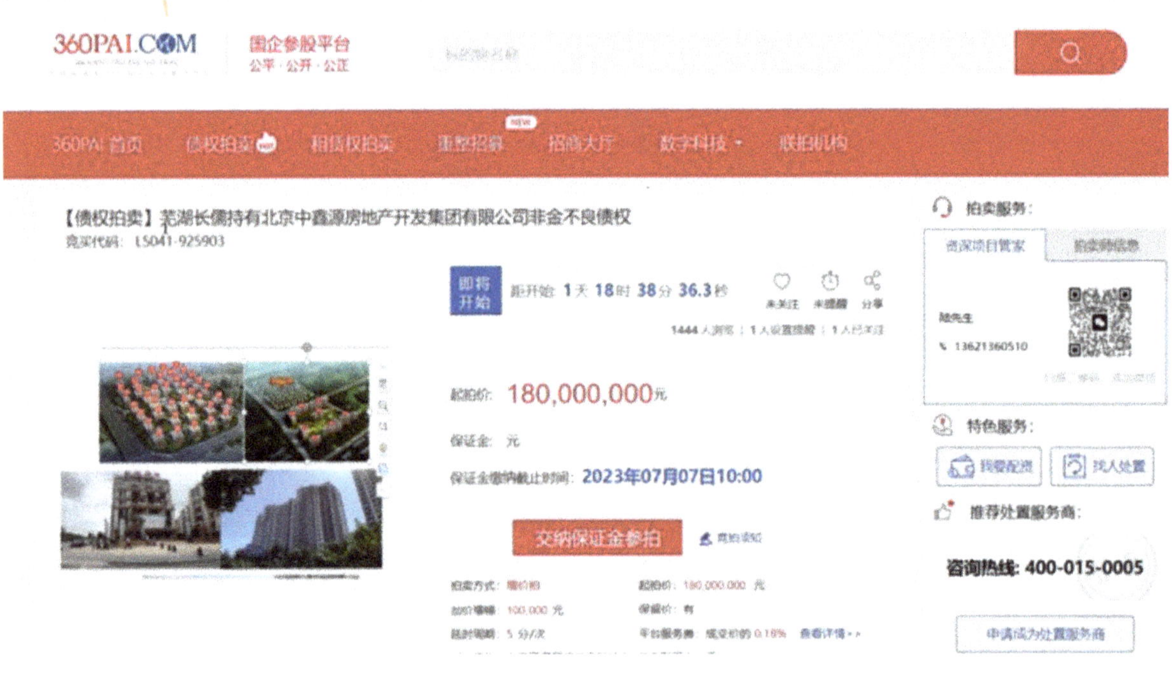

Source: 360pai.com (People's Republic of China).

The OnBid platform is a mature and successful auction platform for asset sales. Its web presentation includes many features typically seen on online marketplaces focused on private individuals. Institutionally focused platforms like nplmarkets.com in Europe or debtx.com in the United States would typically present less detail publicly and distribute extensive information packages including detailed data tapes and access to VDRs only after completion of an institutional onboarding process and signing of a nondisclosure agreement. Figure 17 shows a multi-family building with several attachments including exact location, pictures, maps, land registry excerpts, and valuation reports. The website also provides details about the bidding process such as the number of past failed attempts, the timing of the next auction, reserve prices, and auction and bidding details.

Figure 17: Real Estate Asset for Public Auction on the OnBid Platform

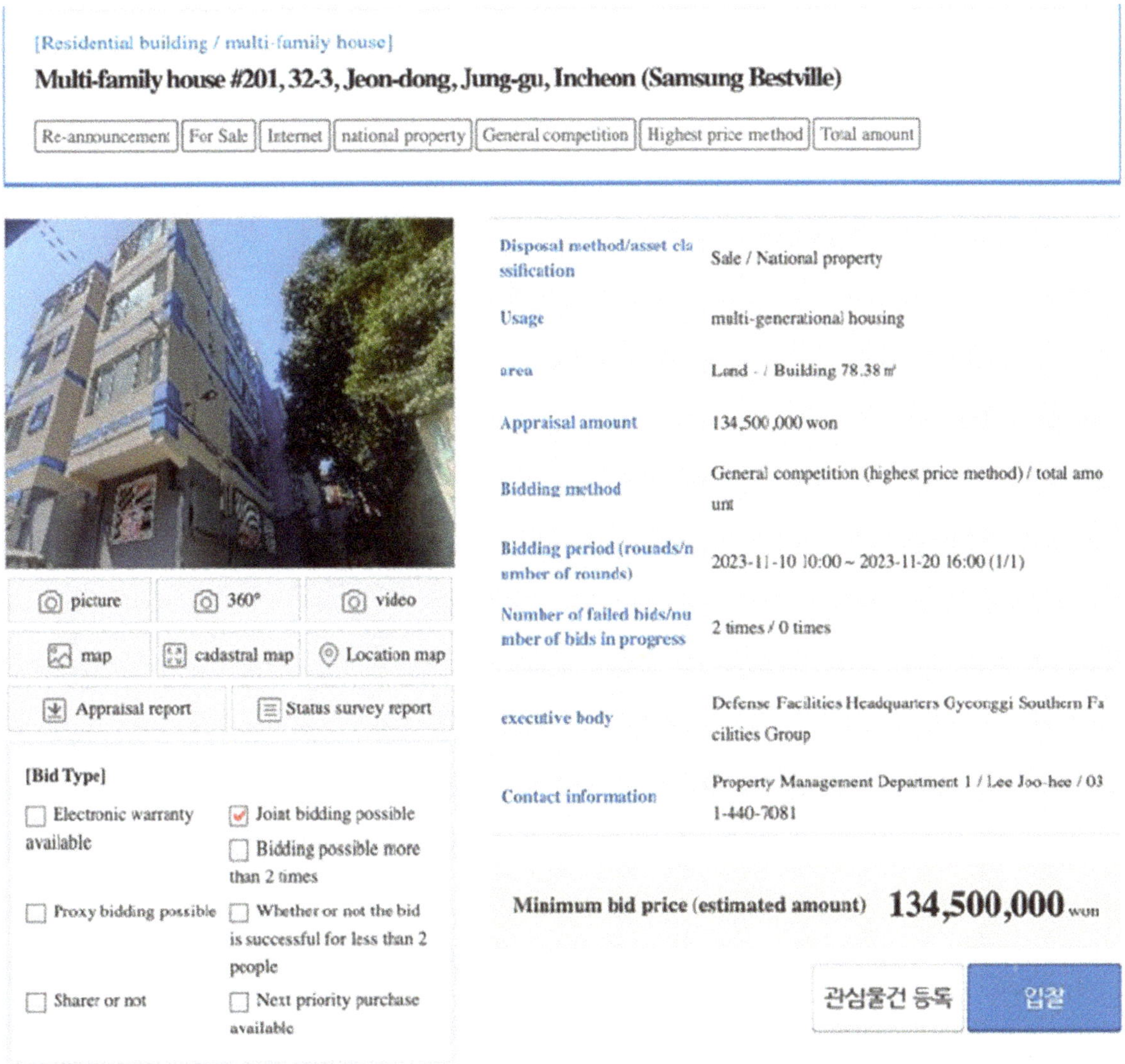

Source: KAMCO OnBid (browser translation by Google Chrome).

Data extraction and loan data tape preparation: The details of structured and unstructured information sets for NPL sales are discussed in Chapter 4. More detail is provided here on the process to extract and create the structured data in the required format. Ideally, the seller's IT systems should allow us to easily gather information on distressed assets to create loan data tapes that cover all essential or mandatory data fields. To extract the required information, the seller must be familiar with the data templates used by the platform and expected by investors. In markets where standard mandatory data templates exist, they take priority in the initial data extraction before supplying additional voluntary information that may help investors to price more aggressively. The seller should review the existing IT system to enable the optimization of the selection process. The seller should set a target perimeter of assets for selection and, if the resulting query returns to many assets, define optimization criteria to shape the target transaction composition. For example, sellers may only select assets of one type to target specific investors, i.e., do not mix unsecured consumer claims with corporate claims or performing with NPLs.

Virtual data room preparation for due diligence: A data room service, nowadays almost exclusively provided in virtual form as a VDR, is an important tool for efficient due diligence, by uploading all supporting standardized or unstructured information on the assets for sale. The VDR due diligence phase is generally the most time-consuming of the transaction process. A well organized and complete VDR enables investors to ask questions and conduct proper financial and legal analysis of the assets. Processes with incomplete data rooms or too aggressive timetables may force investors to make conservative assumptions and lower their price. The electronic and physical transfer of VDR documentation between the winning bidder and the seller is typically arranged on a bilateral basis without involvement of the platform.

Transaction documents (nondisclosure agreement, process letter, sale and purchase agreements): The seller should approve and upload to the platform all required transaction documents. This includes nondisclosure agreement templates to be signed with investors, a process letter describing the different transaction phases, nonbinding offer letters and binding offer letters with details on timing and information requirements in the different bidding phases, and a draft sale and purchase agreement that potential buyers can acknowledge or negotiate prior to bidding. The platform may suggest standardized document templates for the seller's use or let the seller upload their own approved documents.

Complaints procedure: Different disputes require consideration. Disputes related to auction results; disruption of services; complaints and appeals in the auction processes offered by the platform; and suggestions for improving the platform's accessibility, stability, and ease of use. User registration documents should include dispute resolution clauses and the platform should have change management tools and ticketing systems in place to deal with complaints, recommendations for improvement, or bug reports.

5.7.1 Transaction Process Management and Auction Details

The platform execution process should follow the best practice guidance for NPL transactions as explained below. Platforms should align with best practice guidance and local market conventions and must comply with regulations. The platform should support all phases in the transaction execution process from the initial transaction and data preparation, investor onboarding, listing, or marketing, exchanging documents like nondisclosure agreements or process letters and nonbinding or binding offer guidelines to the actual auction and post-auction functions. Figure 18 shows the transaction phases and highlights which necessary actions are performed on the platform.

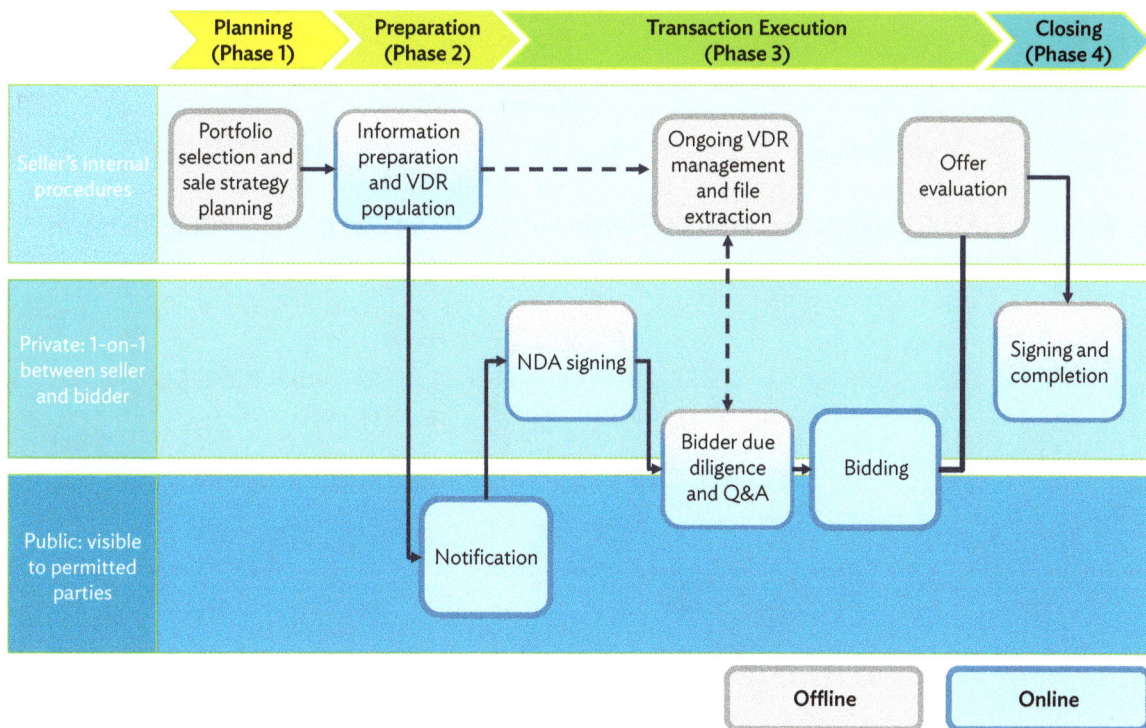

Figure 18: Transaction Process for Trading Nonperforming Loans Online and Offline

NDA = nondisclosure agreement, Q&A = question and answer, VDR = virtual data room.
Source: Deloitte as cited in ADB 2022.

Deal setup: The seller sets up the deal by uploading a teaser presentation, legal documents, a loan data tape and sets the deal and auction calendar, i.e., sets a schedule of the upcoming auction with dates and times and invites buyers. The details of the transaction process can be summarized in a process letter with details on timing and preconditions for buyers to participate in due diligence and auction phases. Buyers are either picked by the seller or are invited based on their interest expression on the listing website. Transactions can be the sale of a single asset, a portfolio of assets or loans that must be sold as one package, or a portfolio of assets or loans that can be sold in one bidding process to different bidders (sometimes called partial bids or bids wanted in competition).

Bidding platform: The platform provides an interface for users to place bids in real time after the seller has set up the transaction on the platform and started the auction. The auction set up includes start and end time, and any extension rules. Other auction features include the selection of the auction method (sealed bid or timed auction using different auction methods like English or Dutch auctions), manual and automated bid increments, setting of a reserve price (the minimum price set by the seller for the asset to be sold), auto bidding where the system places bids on behalf of users up to their set limit, a countdown timer that displays the remaining time of the auction, and the full bid history recording all bids placed during an auction. The platform sends an alert to the highest bidder at the end of the auction and also provides the option to display the winning bid and bidder after the auction concludes. For many institutional sales, the winning bid and bidder may not be disclosed unless required by regulation.

Figure 19 shows an example of a user interface for an electronic auction as seen by the bidder. The auction function clearly states the type of auction (English), the bidding format (Absolute means the prices are in currency, i.e., not a percentage of legal balance as would be required in a forward flow sale agreement), starting time, starting prices, price increments, leading bid, remaining time, and potential extension subject to an extension hurdle.

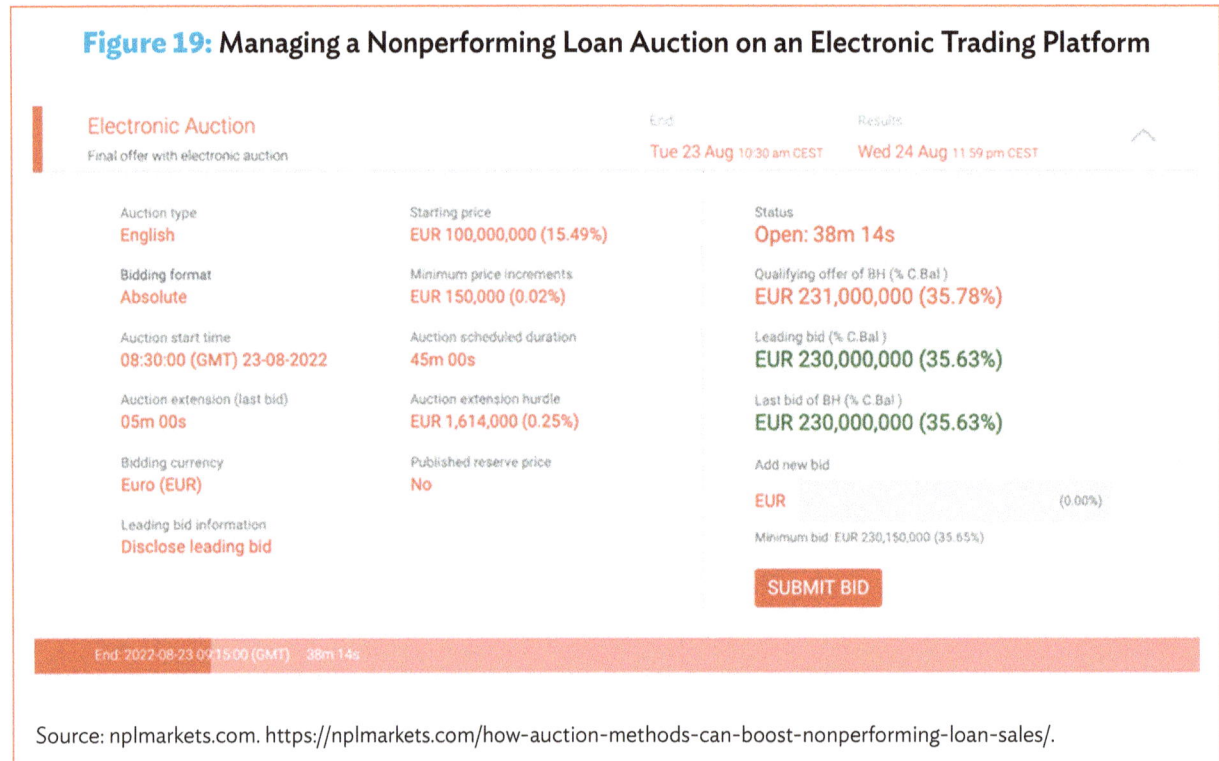

Figure 19: Managing a Nonperforming Loan Auction on an Electronic Trading Platform

Source: nplmarkets.com. https://nplmarkets.com/how-auction-methods-can-boost-nonperforming-loan-sales/.

Ancillary services include full transaction advisory, data preparation, data enrichment and valuation advice, due diligence and VDR services, communication tools, and document exchanges to help facilitate debt trading by providing better analytical and due diligence capacity for a smoother trade execution. These are the most common services provided:

Transactional advisory: Sellers can benefit from professional advice on how to optimally select and structure portfolios and prepare data to be posted in data rooms. The analytics tools provided by some platforms can help find the optimal transaction portfolio based on key performance indicators specific to the seller and impact on the seller's balance sheet.

Data preparation, valuation, and analytics: As discussed in Chapter 4, to narrow the bid–offer gap, valuation services can provide guidance on the market value of assets to be sold. For sellers to access a reliable valuation tool can help them select the most suitable portfolio with the most advantageous impact on the balance sheet.

Stress testing and scenario analysis: Investors and sellers might benefit from tools to evaluate potential risks to their loans via stress testing variables such as collateral values, cash flows, interest rates, and market spreads. Scenario analysis can help investors and sellers to explore parameter sensitivities to key valuation inputs like the discount rate.

Deal closing: Additional assistance can be provided to finalize legal documents such as sales and purchase agreements and ensure a smooth transfer of ownership rights. Standardized legal templates can help in this process. Notifying authorities and borrowers can be important additional tasks supported by the platform.

Reporting: If local or regional transaction regulatory reporting requirements are in place, automatic files can be prepared for authorities or even sent directly to them. Business reporting functions on the platform can be very extensive showing all past cash flows on the assets for sale plus cash flow projections by the seller or third-party advisors such as due diligence advisors or loan servicers engaged by the investor.

5.7.2 Marketing and Sales Strategy for Nonperforming Loan Platforms

Unless the use of the transaction platform is mandated by law or regulation, it is critical that the platform meets the needs of their users and all potential users become aware of it. The following steps can be taken to implement a marketing and sales strategy:

(i) **Identify the target audience:** Identify the target audience for the platform, including potential buyers and sellers of NPLs.

(ii) **Develop a value proposition:** Develop a clear and compelling value proposition that explains why buyers and sellers should use the platform to trade NPLs. This may include benefits such as a wider selection of NPLs, transparent pricing, a streamlined transaction process following best practice guidelines and access to the widest possible network of investors with a detailed understanding of their preferences and investment profiles.

(iii) **Highlight the benefits:** The benefits of using an online trading platform can include greater efficiency, transparency, and access to a wider pool of potential buyers. Sellers may also appreciate the ease and convenience of using an online platform, as it can save time and reduce the need for manual processes.

(iv) **Provide case studies and testimonials:** These can include those from other sellers who have used the platform successfully to illustrate the benefits of using the platform and build trust with potential sellers.

(v) **Build a strong brand:** Develop a strong brand for a platform that is memorable, professional, and trustworthy. This may include developing a logo, color scheme, and other visual elements that reflect the values of the platform.

(vi) **Use targeted advertising:** Use targeted advertising to reach potential buyers and sellers of NPLs. This may include online ads, social media ads, and other forms of digital marketing.

(vii) **Leverage content marketing:** Create content that provides value to potential buyers and sellers of NPLs. This may include blog posts, whitepapers, and case studies that educate users about the benefits of using the platform.

(viii) **Attend industry events:** Conferences and trade shows to network with potential buyers and sellers of NPLs can help build platform awareness and generate leads.

(ix) **Develop referral programs:** These can incentivize existing platform users to refer new buyers and sellers of NPLs and help generate word-of-mouth marketing and build a community around the platform.

(x) **Measure results:** Measure the results of the marketing and sales strategy by tracking key metrics such as website traffic, lead generation, and customer acquisition. Use this data to refine and improve the strategy over time.

(xi) **Leverage industry partnerships:** Partnerships with industry associations, banks, credit institutions, and other financial institutions can build credibility and promote the platform to potential seller.

5.7.3 Best Practice Execution Guidelines

Table 6 summarizes the key steps involved in selling NPL to institutional investors (European Commission 2022). Table 6 shows the general process for a two-phase transaction which includes a non-binding offer phase in addition to the binding offer phase. Both single-phase and two-phase transaction processes are common and should be supported by the platform.

Table 6: Best Practice Execution Guidelines Adopted and Modified from Europe

Phase	Key Activities	Key Deliverables
Portfolio Selection	• Review existing information technology (IT) system • Define transaction perimeter, select the portfolio to sell • Decide upon the use of internal resources vs external platform	• Amend IT system • Select portfolio for sale • Establish organizational structure, sign external contracts
Preparation Phase	• Define process phases with or without Non-Binding Offers (NBOs), set timeline • Prepare all transaction documents (Teaser, Presentation, Info Memo) • Prepare NDAs, Process Letter, Bid Guidelines, Purchase Agreement • Prepare loan data tape, set up VDR	• Virtual data room (VDR), Teaser, Info Memo • Management Presentation • Non-disclosure agreement (NDA), Process Letter, Bid Guidelines • Purchase Agreement • Loan data tape • VDR rules
Premarketing	• Market sounding with investors • Define best marketing strategy • Complete process and marketing docs	• Process Letter • Due Diligence Material • Investor long list, sign NDA
Non-Binding Offer (Phase 1)	• Phase 1 VDR Access • Disclose process materials • Disclose data tapes (in VDR) • Manage Q&A process • Analyze submitted NBOs • Select bidders for the Binding Offer (BO) Phase • Finalize the transaction portfolio	• Prepare Phase 2 VDR • Loan data tapes (full set) • Vendor Due Diligence • VDR reporting (e.g., on bidder activity) • Provide answers in Q&A • Analysis Report of NBOs and shortlist of bidders

continued on next page

Table 6 *continued*

Phase	Key Activities	Key Deliverables
Binding Offer Phase (Phase 2)	• Provide Phase 2 data and documents to Phase 2 investors • Manage of Q&A process • Organize management meeting (if any) • Organize the auction • Analyze submitted BO letters and Loan Sale and Purchase Agreement (LSPA) Mark-Ups. Select preferred bidder.	• Final management presentation • Vendor due diligence reports to Phase 2 Investors • VDR reporting • BO Report and selection of Preferred Bidder
Signing and Closing	• Execute transaction documentation including LSPA • Financial closing • Prepare transfer of data and documents • Accounting of the transaction	• VDR archives • Final LSPA
Post-Closing	• Transfer assets, data, and documents to the purchaser for a smooth on-boarding • Manage seller's responsibilities during liability period as established in the LSPA • Define after-sale activities, regulate the interactions of seller, purchaser, and borrowers during transfer and beyond • Implementation of the obligations of the Purchaser in the management of the portfolios set in the LSPA	

Source: European Commission 2022.

5.8 Ten Steps for Establishing a Platform to Trade Nonperforming Loan

To sum up, there are 10 steps required to establish an online NPL trading platform. As noted, selling portfolios of NPLs is complex and benefits from best practice guidelines, standardized data templates, and advanced platform technology. As buyers and sellers often need advice that requires human interaction with experts and offline process components, a successful online platform will need to find an efficient way to integrate all such components.

(i) **Identify need:** The first step is to identify the need for a platform to trade NPLs. This can be done by conducting market research and identifying potential buyers and sellers of NPLs, as well as any existing platforms in the market.

(ii) **Define the scope:** Scope includes the types of NPLs that will be traded, the target market, the type of investors (private individuals or institutions or both), and the services that will be offered to buyers and sellers. Decide whether the platform is targeted at institutional or retail investors or both.

(iii) **Develop the platform:** Once scope has been defined, develop the platform by building a website and ancillary data, valuation, reporting and due diligence functions. At a minimum the platform should allow buyers and sellers to register, for sellers to upload information about their assets, for investors to see the assets or be invited to transactions once launched, and for sellers and buyers to execute transactions.

(iv) **Analyze the legal framework:** Analyze and design the legal framework that defines the terms and conditions of the platform, including the rights and obligations of buyers and sellers, the fee structure, and the dispute resolution process.

(v) **Build a network of partners:** This network can include credit institutions, AMCs, domestic and international investors, and debt collectors, to provide a steady supply and demand of NPLs for the platform.

(vi) **Implement marketing and sales strategy:** Develop a marketing and sales strategy to attract buyers and sellers to the platform. This may include targeted advertising, social media marketing, and other promotional activities.

(vii) **Ensure legal and regulatory compliance:** Ensure compliance with all relevant laws and regulations governing the trading of NPLs. Establish a rigorous governance framework.

(viii) **Provide customer support:** Provide customer support to buyers and sellers, including a helpdesk, chat support, and other services as needed.

(ix) **Monitor platform performance:** Monitor the performance of the platform by tracking key metrics such as the number of transactions, revenue, and customer satisfaction. Use this data to refine and improve the platform over time.

(x) **Expand the platform:** Once the platform is established and running smoothly, consider expanding it by adding new features, services, and markets.

6 Conclusions

The development of NPL markets in Asia and the Pacific varies significantly across the region. While some countries boast established platforms and trading mechanisms, others require legal reforms to attract investors and ensure efficient NPL resolution. This second ADB feasibility study explores how legal frameworks impact NPL markets and trading platforms, focusing on Viet Nam and the Republic of Korea, and provides technical and operational guidance on establishing online NPL trading platforms.

One key takeaway is the crucial role of online platforms in connecting buyers and sellers, fostering market efficiency, and bridging information gaps. These platforms can attract foreign investors and improve pricing transparency, ultimately contributing to a more robust NPL market. B2C platforms in countries like the Republic of Korea and the PRC have demonstrated success in overcoming valuation challenges for individual assets like properties, leveraging their large user bases and dominant market positions.

However, for economies grappling with high NPL volumes, efficient portfolio sales are critical. B2B platforms can facilitate the sale of large NPL portfolios to institutional investors. These platforms go beyond simply connecting buyers and sellers, often offering value-added services such as investor databases, data preparation, valuation tools, and data hubs.

Standardization plays a crucial role in streamlining NPL transactions. In this study, ADB proposes a standardized data template to ensure clear and consistent information exchange between buyers and sellers across jurisdictions.

Finally, the importance of high-quality data cannot be overstated. Overcoming information asymmetry, a key challenge in NPL markets, requires a comprehensive data ecosystem encompassing investor profiles, historical cash flows, and transaction prices. Better data can help overcome bid–offer spreads. Government agencies can establish central data hubs and harvest the information already available in the reporting to bank supervisors, central banks, and central credit registers. By promoting better data collection and utilization, stakeholders can enhance market efficiency and pave the way for a more robust NPL market in Asia and the Pacific.

References

Asian Development Bank (ADB). 2022. Road Map for Developing an Online Platform to Trade Nonperforming Loans in Asia and the Pacific. Manila. https://www.adb.org/publications/road-map-online-platform-trade-nonperforming-loans.

Deloitte. 2023. Deleveraging Asia. Preparing for the Next Wave, Q2–2023. https://www2.deloitte.com/content/dam/Deloitte/sg/Documents/finance/sea-fa-deleveraging-asia-q2-2023.pdf.

European Banking Authority (EBA). Implementing Technical Standards on NPL Transaction Data Templates. https://www.eba.europa.eu/legacy/regulation-and-policy/regulatory-activities/credit-risk/implementing-technical-standards-npl.

European Commission (EC). 2022. Guidelines for a Best-Execution Process for Sales of Nonperforming Loans on Secondary Markets. C(2022) 7277 final. Brussels.

Fell, J., M. Grodzicki, D. Krušec, R. Martin, and E. O'Brien. 2017. Overcoming Nonperforming Loan Market Failures with Transaction Platforms. *Financial Stability Review*. 2(1). pp 130–144.

Fischetto, A. L., I. Guida, A. Rendina, and G. Santini. 2022. Notes on Financial Stability and Supervision. No. 32, 2022—Bad Loan Recovery Rates in 2021. Bank of Italy, Rome.

Hoang Quan Appraisal. 2022. Government Regulations on the Valuation of the Starting Price for Bad Debt Auctions. https://www.hqa.com.vn/government-regulations-on-valuation-the-starting-of-bad-debts.html.

International Finance Corporation (IFC). 2022. Presentation on Entry Barriers to the NPL Debt Trading Market in Viet Nam. Washington, DC.

International Monetary Fund (IMF). 2023. *World Economic Outlook, October 2023: Navigating Global Divergences*. Washington, DC: IMF.

Korea Asset Management Corp. (KAMCO). 2022. NPL Securitization. Presentation at the VAMC Workshop on Developing the NPL Trading Market in Viet Nam. Presented by Sunjoon Choe.

KPMG. 2023. Methodological Report for the Creation of an Electronic Platform for the Sale of Distressed Assets in Kazakhstan.

NPL Markets. 2020. Italian NPL ABS Cash Flow Projections. https://nplmarkets.com/italian-npl-abs-cash-flow-projections/.

——. 2023a. Final Draft Implementing Technical Standards from EBA for NPL Transaction Data Templates. https://nplmarkets.com/final-draft-implementing-technical-standards-from-eba-for-npl-transaction-data-templates/.

——. 2023b. Lessons Learnt from First EBA NPL Data Templates. 16 March. https://nplmarkets.com/lessons-learnt-from-first-eba-npl-data-templates/.

Pelizza, M. and K. R. Schenk-Hoppé. 2020. Pricing Defaulted Italian Mortgages. *Journal of Risk and Financial Management*. 13(2). pp 1–14. ISSN 1911-8074, MDPI, Basel.

State Bank of Vietnam (SBV). 2022. Developing NPL Trading Market to Help Resolve NPLs. https://www.sbv.gov.vn/webcenter/portal/m_en/home/sbv/news/news_chitiet?leftWidth=0%25&showFooter=fa.

World Bank. 2021. *Nonperforming Loans in East Asia and the Pacific: Practices and Lessons in Times of COVID-19*. Washington, DC: World Bank.

————. 2022. Asset Sale Practices and Use of Electronic Debt Trading Platforms by Public Asset Management Companies and Deposit Insurance Funds. VAMC Report 2022. Washington, DC.

————. 2022. Electronic Debt Trading Platform of VAMC Report.

Zheshang Asset Research Institute. 2023. Success Factors and Case Studies of Online Platforms in China. https://upload.congkong.net/ipaf/pdf/s7b.pdf.